Play and Friendship in Inclusive Autism Education

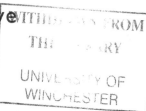

Taking an innovative approach to autism and play, this practical text focuses on the particular form play and friendship take for children with autism and their peers. Autistic children have clear preferences for play, with sensory-perceptual experience remaining a strong feature as they develop. *Play and Friendship in Inclusive Autism Education* offers a framework for supporting children's development through play, with step-by-step guidance on how to facilitate the playful engagement of children with autism.

Up-to-date research findings and relevant theoretical ideas are presented in an accessible and practical way, highlighting what theory means to ordinary practice in schools, whilst focusing on practical knowledge in autism education. Organised into five chapters, this book covers some of the main issues surrounding inclusive education and play:

- discourses and definitions of play
- the difference between play and playfulness
- autism, play and the inclusion agenda in education
- the nature of sensory-perceptual experience in children's play cultures
- effective ways of supporting children's friendships.

With practical guidance on how to support children with autism through play, this book will be essential reading for teachers, learning support assistants, SENCos and play workers, as well as professionals working in an advisory capacity. Students studying courses that cover autism will also find *Play and Friendship in Inclusive Autism Education* a valuable resource.

Carmel Conn is a Senior Lecturer in Special Educational Needs at the University of South Wales, UK.

Play and Friendship in Inclusive Autism Education

Supporting learning and development

Carmel Conn

Routledge
Taylor & Francis Group

LONDON AND NEW YORK

First published 2016
by Routledge
2 Park Square, Milton Park, Abingdon, Oxon OX14 4RN

and by Routledge
711 Third Avenue, New York, NY 10017

Routledge is an imprint of the Taylor & Francis Group, an informa business

British Library Cataloguing in Publication Data
A catalogue record for this book is available from the British Library

Library of Congress Cataloging-in-Publication Data
Names: Conn, Carmel, author.
Title: Play and friendship in inclusive autism education : supporting learning and
    development / Carmel Conn.
Description: New York : Routledge, 2016. | Includes bibliographical references
    and index.
Identifiers: LCCN 2015035175 | ISBN 9781138842120 (hardback : alk. paper) |
    ISBN 9781138842137 (pbk. : alk. paper) | ISBN 9781315731810 (ebook)
Subjects: LCSH: Autistic children—Education—Social aspects. | Autistic
    children—Recreation. | Play—Social aspects. | Inclusive education—
    Social aspects.
Classification: LCC LC4717.5 .C66 2016 | DDC 371.9—dc23
LC record available at http://lccn.loc.gov/2015035175

ISBN: 978-1-138-84212-0 (hbk)
ISBN: 978-1-138-84213-7 (pbk)
ISBN: 978-1-315-73181-0 (ebk)

Typeset in Sabon
by Apex CoVantage, LLC
Printed in Great Britain by
Ashford Colour Press Ltd, Gosport, Hants

MIX
Paper from
responsible sources
FSC® C011748
www.fsc.org

Contents

Figures

Tables

Preface

The two books in this series, *Observation, Assessment and Planning in Inclusive Autism Education: Supporting Learning and Development* and *Play and Friendship in Inclusive Autism Education: Supporting Learning and Development*, have the aim of presenting an educationally relevant and inclusive approach to supporting autistic pupils in schools. At present, the field of autism education is dominated by specialist practices that are strongly influenced by a medical model of individual difference and deficit. Many of these are hard to implement in ordinary classrooms and serve to exclude autistic pupils from the outset. These books seek to provide an alternative approach to educating pupils with autism, one that promotes observation-based pedagogy, partnership working and respect for difference and diversity. Reflection on children's learning and everyday experiences at school – practitioners sharing their reflections with others, including parents and pupils – is at the heart of these processes and is seen to be what underpins best practice in autism education.

Children's learning and development are located within social contexts and involve social processes that are transactional in nature. Within both these books, a sociocultural perspective on pupil learning is taken, which views the child or young person within an environment that includes other people's communication, understandings and ways of interacting. Inclusive autism education is described as an interactive process of teaching and learning that is embedded within social relationships and involves situated learning. The view put forward is that education should be less concerned with individual psychology and more with developing rich contexts for learning that support the participation of all pupils.

Importantly, a sociocultural perspective is concerned with patterns of behaviour and what is shared within communities of practice, but also with seeing the value in difference and diversity. Locating learning and development within the sociocultural environment requires withholding judgements about what pupils know and can do until a proper understanding of pupils' experiences and ways of making sense of situations is gained. This involves taking steps to gain information about pupils' perspectives and giving them a voice within the teaching and learning process. It also involves practitioners, pupils and parents reflecting on the understandings, beliefs and values they bring to contexts of learning, and making appropriate adjustments following these reflections. A sociocultural perspective on autism is of interest to the progressive practitioner who wants to develop their practice and find new ways of supporting children and young people.

Up-to-date research findings and relevant theoretical ideas are presented in both books in accessible and practical ways. Since autism education is concerned with what is most fundamental in human development – that is, communication and social sharing – an interdisciplinary approach is used. Understandings from developmental psychology are discussed within parts of the text, but these are presented alongside ideas taken from other disciplines, including childhood studies and disability studies. An educational perspective is interwoven throughout as a way of aligning research with practice, ensuring that ways of working and forms of support are always oriented towards ordinary teaching and learning processes. It should be noted that an interdisciplinary approach provides practitioners and parents with a greater understanding of children's social worlds and enables them to see what is different in the behaviour of autistic pupils, but also ways in which these pupils are the same. It enables them to see what belongs to the individual, but also what is part of group processes, what are the pupil's social difficulties and learning needs, but also what are the pupil's strengths and important interests.

The intention here is to highlight what theory means to ordinary practice in schools, but the emphasis is on the central importance of practical knowledge in autism education. Practical knowledge is the everyday understandings that practitioners hold about the pupils with whom they work, and the knowledge about their child that parents contribute too. Ways of working and forms of learning support promoted in these books are 'bottom-up' in the sense that they centrally use people's practical knowledge – that is, knowledge of *specific* interactions and relationships, features of *particular* learning environments and *unique* personal experiences. Inclusive autism education is more concerned with children's actual social experiences, interactions and relationships – and less with generalized ideas about what these might or should be – and this fact makes practical knowledge the starting point in teaching and learning.

The ways in which we choose to describe phenomena is critically important to how we understand it. A strongly medicalized discourse dominates autism theory and practice at present. This uses a normative discourse and describes autistic children in terms of their 'deficits'. A further aim of the two books in this series is to help to insert another form of words into discussions about autistic children, their play, interactions and friendships, and their education, learning and development. To this end, terminology use is carefully considered throughout. Person-first language (i.e. child with autism) and the terms 'autistic child' and 'autistic pupil' are both used here. This is used respectfully to reflect current professional language use, but also the preference of some people in the autistic community who see person-first language and its use only where a characteristic is viewed negatively, as contributing to the construction of negative identities (Sinclair, 2009).

Chapter 1

What is play?

Focus of this chapter:

- discourses and definitions of play
- the purposes of play, including its importance to the development of the social brain, as participation in socioculture, as physical activity and as a creative space away from real life
- the nature of children's play, making reference to its significance in terms of child development but also its everyday value in supporting children's interactions with each other
- categories of children's play
- difficult issues in relation to play, including play as a context for social exclusion.

Introduction

The word 'play' is a deceptively simple term for what is widely acknowledged to be a complex and multifaceted phenomenon. We know that play is carried out by humans and animals, adults and children, and that it takes many different forms, but we do not fully know the purpose of play or why it develops in the way it does. The purpose of play has been described from both evolutionary and socio-historical perspectives, and as a feature of learning and development, as emotional experience and as contributing to the growth of self (Göncü and Gaskins, 2006). Different theories of play have been developed, but often these focus on only one aspect of play rather than take in 'the whole picture'. The complexity of play reflects the complexity of human behaviour itself, which is determined by multiple influences that are in dynamic and interactive relationship. However, play helps to reveal the fact that understanding human behaviour and development involves understanding our biological materiality as well as and in critical relation to social and cultural processes.

The dominance of developmental psychology in autism theory and practice has meant that a narrow view of autism and play has prevailed. This takes a strongly cognitive view, one that sees the development of play as straightforwardly linked to intellectual development. Forms of play that are seen to be cognitively relevant, most important amongst these being pretend play, are prioritised, whilst other types of play are overlooked. Consistent with this view is that play for the neurotypically developing child is a behaviour that relates to their cognitive development, much more than to – or even in isolation from – the sociocultural world. Within the literature on autism, the development of play has been conceptualized as a set of skills to be learned or a series of actions to be performed, with little sense that play exists as the result of the child's intrinsic motivation and interactive responses with the world around.

Mastrangelo (2009) amongst other writers has remarked on the oddness of the approach to play in autism, where children's play is seen to involve adult direction, involuntary action, goal orientation and adult determination of play materials. However, as Sutton-Smith (1997) points out in his definitive work on the meaning of play, this moulding of ideas about play to suit the particular discourse or 'rhetoric' of an academic discipline has been a feature of play scholarship since the 1800s. Many theories of play highlight one purpose and focus on this to the exclusion of other features of play, which are dismissed as irrelevant or not 'proper play'. The cognitive developmental discourse that dominates autism theory is served by a view of play that sees it as contributing to growth and intellectual development in the neurotypical case and a defining 'deficit skill' in autism. Such a narrow view results in a diminution in our overall understanding of what play is, how it may exist differentially for people with autism, and how carers and professionals can support play in children's lives.

In this chapter and in the one that follows, understandings about play, its purpose and the many forms it takes in ordinary contexts will be explored as a way of providing a wide perspective on play. It is hoped that this will serve to provide a useful starting point for thinking about autism and play and how we can support children's learning and development through play, which are the subjects of the last three chapters in this book.

Definition of play

A comprehensive and widely used definition of play is that found in Caillois's classic text, *Man, Play and Games* (1958/2001). According to this definition, behaviour can be described as play if it involves the following criteria:

- it is a free and voluntary act, one that is intrinsically motivated and not externally prompted;
- it involves joy, amusement, absorption and other aspects of positive feeling;

- there is an outcome that is unproductive and cannot be predicted in advance;
- it relates to the time and culture in which the play takes place;
- it involves a duality of the player's personal style, concerns and interpretations alongside rules and other limitations for certain types of games.

In defining play, Caillois provided four classifications of play to encompass all the different forms and functions of play. He described play as essentially organized into the following: competitions and games of contest, games of chance or luck, play that involves mimicry and imagination, and a special form of locomotor play that Caillois described as 'dizzy play'. This last classification is interesting because it refers to play that brings a momentary disruption of perception and voluntarily inflicted 'panic state of mind' – for example, the experience of play involved in swinging upside down or spinning round and round. Caillois describes dizzy play as 'without thought', but it could also be viewed as an unusually non-social, physical form of play in its orientation.

Caillois pointed out that categories of play often exist in combined forms – for example, imaginative role play games that involve a contest, as in playfighting, or sporting activity that involves elements of luck, as in horse racing. He also saw play as something that adults do as well as children, describing sport, physical contest, performance, the arts and many other everyday leisure activities as adult forms of play.

Sutton-Smith's (1997) more recent and highly influential treatise on play also takes a wide view of play, seeing it as something that describes adult as well as children's behaviour. He describes play as having wide parameters that encompass a diversity of activity, including mental 'play', such as daydreaming, solitary activities, such as reading, the playful behaviour involved in playing tricks on someone, organized social activity, such as playing or watching sport, engaging in performance, celebrations, festivals and contests, and 'risky activity', such as extreme sports. Sutton-Smith argues that the diversity of play makes variability its defining characteristic. He sees play as a form of communication that is loaded with adaptive potential and powerfully argues that play probably serves many purposes. For Sutton-Smith, theories of play largely reflect the perspective of the theorist and their particular interests, with no one academic discipline able to fully describe the meaning of play.

The multiple purposes of play

Play has been described according to theories of evolution, development, education, socioculture and anthropology, and as therapeutic support. The intrinsic and voluntary nature of play, taken together with the fact that it is not unique to human beings but also exists in other animal species, has meant that it has been seen as having some evolutionary purpose, though recent theories of play have given this view less prominence (Burghardt, 2005). Behaviours seen in play are often similar to those that exist in real life, and this once led to the belief that play is a form of adaptive behaviour. Play was viewed as a process of trying out actions, interactions and movements, taking risks and making mistakes, and so as a training for life. It was believed that important skills needed for unpredictable or more dangerous situations are rehearsed within a safe play space, where adverse responses and reactions are minimal. Playfighting was seen as a key skill in this respect, human and animal players acting out aggression in ways that feel close to real life whilst being recognized as not actually real (Bateson, 1972).

In recent years, empirical research into play, both animal play and play in human beings, has not supported this idea of play as practice for life. Play behaviour often differs from the way in which humans conduct themselves in real-life situations. For example, play tends to be highly repetitive and dissimilar in this respect to the flexible and constantly changing way in which real-life interaction unfolds. Play often reverses the sequence in which things are done in actuality, fragmenting and punctuating ordinary activity in ways that involve exaggerated gesture, movement and emotion. It is also the case that repetition in play does not reduce as a skill is learned and appears to be done more for the sake of the excitement and pleasure involved. Moreover, some behaviour, such as fighting, exists in species that do not have playfighting in their play repertoire. For other species, it may be the males who carry out the playfighting whilst the females do the real fighting (Sutton-Smith, 1997). There is also no evidence that the amount of play increases the player's ability to perform a corresponding real-life skill (Lillard et al., 2013). Children who play in only small amounts, for example, are not necessarily less able to use language, be creative or problem-solve in later life.

Consideration of cultural differences in relation to play also casts doubt on the idea of play as having evolutionary purpose. Though much of the research into human play has been carried out in Western societies, it is nevertheless apparent that play does not exist in the same way in different cultures. Play is highly variable and exists unequally in different societies. Some cultures do not recognize or encourage children's play and may provide much less time for play. Adults within one society view children's play in different ways too, some seeing value and learning, and others a set of negative or challenging behaviours that require criticism and control.

In current understandings of the purposes of play, the focus of attention has shifted away from notions of play as evolutionary inheritance. The importance of playful interactions to the development of the social brain is recognized, but less as a single trigger for the development of specific cognitive capacities and more as part of a 'heterogeneous assembly' of biological and social processes that are closely interlinked and mutually determining (Prout, 2005). Ideas about the developmental purpose of play are complemented by recent interest in play as a form of participation in socioculture, particularly for children, whose playful activity involves making sense of and reproducing social interactions and cultural ideas that relate to the world around. Children's playful interactions are increasingly seen as an important way in which they engage socially, particularly with each other. Play as a form of physical activity and play as an expression of self are further areas of interest associated with the purpose of play, which are discussed more fully ahead.

Play and the development of mind

Despite extensive research into play and development, it remains uncertain whether there is a direct causal relationship between the child's ability to play and their development of specific cognitive capacities (Lillard et al., 2013). It appears to be much more the case that play is part of a developmental package, one that involves social sharing, positive emotional states, feelings of safety, self-regulation and quality of care for healthy outcomes. Studies in affective neuroscience and psychobiology suggest that the playful interaction patterns that occur early on in a child's life serve the vital purpose of building healthy neural development and an architecture of the mind (Hobson, 1990). The extended period of human childhood, that is considerably longer than for other primates, is thought to be for the purpose of lengthening the experience of care for the young infant and therefore time spent in affective interaction with their caregiver. Early social-emotional experiences of relationships, which are characterised by repeated, rhythmic experiences of playful interaction, support the child's ability to thrive (Panksepp, 2013). Playful engagement takes the form of seeking out enjoyable alignments of face, voice and body, which is not led by the adult nor by the infant, but takes the form of a kind of dance between the two (Stern, 1985). It is thought that these protracted experiences of social sharing and intense relatedness with another person's mind and body support the development of the capacity to take a thinking stance upon the world, where thought is removed from immediate perceptions and always filtered through a socially driven 'intersubjective' awareness (Hobson, 2002).

Certainly, for educational purposes, play is something that educators recognize as having value, experience presented in playful ways producing much greater impact on learning than didactic teaching. In early years education, play is increasingly seen as a critical context for children's development and a good fit for the highly integrated and affective ways in which children learn. Play supports children to engage with their environment, make sense of experience and express their ideas and feelings. In recent policy statements, most prominent of which is Article 31 of the UN Convention on the Rights of the Child (UN General Assembly, 1989), there has been the introduction of a strong agenda of children's right to play and a recognition of play as an important cultural, artistic and leisure activity for children.

Play and children's participation in socioculture

Ideas about the developmental purpose of play are complemented by sociological theories of childhood that focus on the here-and-now importance of play in children's lives. Investigation into children's spontaneous, everyday social experiences highlights the ways in which play allows them to be active participants in their lives, communicating, cooperating and sharing their ideas and concerns through playful encounters with others and the world around. In play, children bring their knowledge and experience of the world and all their social and cultural understandings, reproducing and transforming these to suit their and others' interests and concerns (Corsaro, 2011). Engaging in play allows children to function optimally in children's social worlds. Playing hones children's social competency and enables them to function better as themselves in the here and now, to present themselves in different ways, engage with other people and be 'the best they can be as a child' (Lester and Russell, 2010). In this way, the child's capacity to participate in play also supports development.

Play suits the ways in which children communicate, which is different from adults and much less verbally based. Children communicate mostly in non-verbal ways, through movement, gesture, sound, posture, facial expression and their use of space. The physical, multimodal and performative forms of communication that are strongly present in children's play match these natural ways of communicating and allow children maximum agency in their social participation and reproduction of culture. However, it should be remembered that play as a form of participation in socioculture varies, depending on the social and cultural contexts of play. Play must be seen as relating to regional and national influences as well as to structures that exist in relation to gender, ethnicity and class. Alongside these three categories, the experience of disability should also be seen as an influencing factor in children's lives (Goodley and Runswick-Cole, 2011). In other words, play relates to the world around and should be viewed as culturally and contextually specific.

Play and physical activity

The physical benefits of play are an aspect of play that has been largely overlooked, but more recently viewed with increasing interest. Many types of play involve vigorous physical activity, such as running, jumping, lifting, pushing, pulling and climbing. Physical or locomotor play is viewed as having the primary purpose of raising the individual's metabolic rate and differs in this respect from social play, such as rough and tumble, which has physical features but is also highly interactive (Pellegrini, 2011). Like other forms of play, physical play is often used in a combined way, where play includes two or more elements – for example, fantasy play that involves pretence alongside physical activity, or games of contest that involve physical play and competition. Physical play varies therefore in terms of how social it is, and can be more or less social – or mostly non-social – depending on the way in which the play is performed.

Physical play is strongly present in early childhood, the rhythmic kicking and bouncing of babies being an early form of this type of play. It is an activity that peaks in four- and five-year-olds, though may continue in some form thereafter for some children (Pellegrini and Smith, 1998). Boys engage more in physical play than girls, and it can be a feature of male cultures in later years too. However, both genders carry out this kind of play and there is increasing recognition that physical play has an important developmental purpose, encouraging motor control, body strength, endurance and economy of movement, whilst also providing vital breaks from cognitive processing.

Play as a separate time and space

One further possible purpose of play is to provide an activity separate from real life and a creative space for personal expression. This perspective on play is supported by the fact that, in play, the process of playing supersedes any product that is made and that play itself has no actual goal. It occurs only when the individual is in a 'relaxed field' and a safe enough space where basic needs relating to food and security have been already met (Burghardt, 2011). As discussed earlier, play behaviour is different from that found in real life, making an exaggerated use of space, employing a greater amount of social referencing and much more repetition. Some theorists of play have put forward the idea that play essentially concerns the creative exploration of ideas and emotions, providing the individual with a time and space away from life for positive expressions of self. Prominent amongst these theorists is Donald Winnicott (1971), who thought that play for both children and adults concerns an experience of psychological well-being and positive sense of self. Play is inherently associated with feelings of pleasure, keen interest and spontaneity, what Winnicott described as a state of being truly alive. For Winnicott, play provides an experience of simply 'being', one that allows the development of a 'true self' and healthy capacity in the individual to relate both to themselves and the world around.

This view of play underpins its use as a form of therapeutic support for mental health and well-being. Play is seen as a vehicle for creative expression and the working out of difficult thoughts and feelings, which can be accompanied by experiences of positive relatedness with another person within the therapeutic space. However, the concept of 'flow' (Csikszentmihalyi, 1992/2002), which has attracted a good deal of attention in recent years, concerns the idea that play-type activity supports everyday well-being for all individuals. Flow describes the state of happiness that is associated with intense personal involvement in a pleasurable activity or relationship and is seen as an experience of creativity that supports an optimum state of being. In some conceptualizations of play, it is a described as a flow activity that produces happiness, contentment and a healthy sense of self for both adults and children.

 Reflective task

Collect photographs of children playing, perhaps taken from children's play encounters in your setting. Try to collect examples of as many different types of play as you can.

Taking each photograph in turn, discuss what forms of play are evident in what children are doing. Think about how children combine different forms of play within play encounters and discuss whether this is what children are doing.

Children's play

Children's play is to some degree distinguishable from adult play since it has its own features that are influenced by the traditions of childhood as well as by children's differing competencies and concerns. Children's play involves recognizable and sometimes age-old practices that have permanence within childhood, but it also concerns novelty, innovation and the creation of new play practices. As children play, they draw on existing culture, norms and routines, but they also produce new cultural expressions, ideas and ways of being. Contemporarily, children's media culture is particularly relevant in this respect, representing a strong influence on children's games and interactions, but also supporting innovative imagined realities and creative play ideas.

Forms and features of children's play differ depending on the context. Whether children are playing at home, in their local neighbourhood, in organized clubs or at school, this will determine to some extent what they play and how they go about playing it. The forms of play that dominate, the way in which children organize themselves and participate within in a group, and structures such as gender, age, ethnicity and disability can all operate differently in different settings. For those of us supporting play in schools, Willett's (2013) classification of playground games may be useful in thinking about children's play in a school setting. Typical playground games can be described in relation to their verbal or physical content in the following way:

- games with *high verbal content* – for example, games with stories, singing games, jokes, riddles, games involving made-up words;
- games with *high verbal and physical content* – for example, games involving singing and dance moves, clapping games;
- games with *high imaginative content* – for example, superhero play, playing mums and dads or families;
- games with *high physical content with equipment* – for example, skipping, ball games, football;
- games with *high physical content without equipment* – for example, tagging games, chasing games, races;
- games involving *body play* – for example, shadow play, Chinese burns, making rude noises with the body.

Understanding children's play: Children as beings and becomings

Play is complex and diverse, and it is often difficult for those outside of a play situation to know and understand the experience of play for the players. This is particularly the case for adults, who are often puzzled by what children are doing in their play. For educational practitioners, who witness children's interactive, fast-paced and unfolding play scenarios on an everyday basis in playgrounds and classrooms, play can feel incomprehensible at times and hard to know how to support.

Understanding children's play is complicated by the fact that it has been viewed largely as having developmental purpose only: that children engage in play in order to move through stages of intellectual growth. Certain forms of play – by far the most important of these being pretend play – have been privileged as 'real play', whilst other forms of play are seen as not relevant. For example, some aspects of children's play, such as their jokes, jeers and loud play, may be viewed by adults as 'silly behaviour'. Other behaviour, such as rough and tumble and vigorous aspects of physical play, may be seen as a challenge to adult authority and something to be controlled. Adults mostly overlook some of children's play, such as when they make rude noises with their bodies, talk gibberish and play with junk media culture. However, recognizing only some behaviour as 'play' means that large amounts of children's everyday activity remain unconceptualized for those adults who seek to understand and support children. When working with children in a school setting, it can feel odd at times to be focusing on only certain aspects of play when it is apparent that children are doing so much more in their interactions.

Sociological theories of childhood have tried to address this narrow view of children's play that sees it as having developmental purpose only by presenting a wider and more encompassing perspective on children's everyday play and playful interactions. These theories see children not as 'passive recipients' of developmental forces but as active participants in their own lives, contributing to and helping to shape the social processes that influence their development. Children are viewed as social actors who actively try to make sense of the world and use these social understandings to navigate their way through their social worlds (James et al., 1998). Play provides a platform which allows children to do this and so supports their emerging competencies and understandings. In play, children construct social identities and reproduce culture as a way of making sense of the world and representing themselves within it.

In an effort to more fully conceptualize what children do on a day-to-day basis and reconcile developmental and sociocultural perspectives on children's activity, including play, Qvortrup (1994) has introduced the idea of children as 'beings' and 'becomings'. Children are 'beings' in that they are actively engaged in day-to-day social processes, but they are also 'becomings' because they are in the process of developing. Thus, children's play is defined by development, but it also has everyday value in how children construct themselves socially and find ways of 'being', by themselves and with others. Box 1.1 describes one child, Ben, aged 8, whose favourite form of play is football, which he plays regularly with his friends at school. This play serves a developmental purpose in that Ben has good coordination skills and physical stamina, but there is social purpose within the play too. The regular arrangement to play football supports social interactions within the group and helps to confirm friendships, and the way in which he and his peers 'perform' as footballers in regular games of football supports children's learning about what is appropriate behaviour for particular social groups.

Box 1.1   Ben plays football with his friends

Ben likes to play football when he can at playtime, which takes place in the field beside the playground. His school does not allow football to be played as a game during morning break, and at this time Ben usually plays other ball games, such as dodgeball and tag with a ball. Ben often asks other boys in his class if they are going to be on the field at break time – that is, that they are also planning to play football. This is an important way in which he confirms his friendships and the ongoing existence of a loose friendship group. Some boys are regulars like Ben and say they will, and others play football only some of the time. Ben and the other boys have been watching the FIFA World Cup on television. When they play football at school, their actions mimic those of the World Cup football players. The boys try to control the ball by catching it first on their chest, try to weave skilfully around other players, and stop the ball suddenly with one foot in order to change their direction of travel. It is apparent that Ben and the other boys admire these skills in each other and recognize the pretence that they too are part of a group of 'professional world class players'.

Adopting an integrated view of play – one that sees play as associated with both being and becoming – helps us to understand that all children's playful activity is of relevance and one of the most important ways in which they engage with each other and their environment. Whether pretence, physical play, playfighting, silly behaviour or rude jokes, children's play and playful interactions reveal the many ways in which they interpret the world and use these interpretations to demonstrate their social competencies and construct themselves as social beings.

Conceptualizing children as beings and becomings means we can understand too how play contains patterns of behaviour that exist across different childhoods, but also great individual variation within these. Not all children play in the same way, some engaging in large amounts of play and others in less play. All children have their preferences in play, and many enjoy physical types of play over play, for example, with a high verbal content. Play reflects gender, race and cultural influences, but is also shaped by momentary events, such as the weather or the news. Children's differing competencies are a further extremely important influence on play and also underpin the differences between children in play and the diversity of play itself.

Play should always be contextualised in terms of the influences that are present for particular groups of children and practices that are present within specific play communities. In thinking about the variation that exists in children's play, it is helpful to consider the different categories of play that exist, which are set out ahead.

Categories of play

Play is notoriously difficult to define. Part of the reason for this is that it exists in many different forms, but a further reason is that play is often carried out multimodally – that is, different types of play are combined within one play scenario. Children's play is very often multimodal on an everyday basis. For example, boys often engage in superhero play that has combined elements of physical play in the form of running and chasing, rough and tumble in the form of playfighting and karate moves, construction play if they create weapons, and a pretend narrative. Similarly, skipping is an activity predominantly carried out by girls and involves physical play, singing and dance moves, and perhaps an element of competition or rule-based play. Even games such as football, which seems to be clearly a physical game, may be more or less about competition and may also include elements of pretence, with players acting out 'being footballers'.

In order to be able to support children in their play, it is helpful to understand the basic categories of play. Different categorisations of play are available, but the play categories identified by Miller and Almon (2009) are particularly useful when thinking about autism and play. These include forms of play with which autistic children are more likely to engage, and the following is an adapted list taken from their outline of categories of play.

1. Sensory play

Examples: *water play, sand play, bubbles, pop-up toys, melting things, spinning objects, reflected light, gentle body movement.*

Sensory play concerns playing with the properties of an object, such as its shape, sound, smell, weight or movement. Sensory play stands in contrast to social play since it involves playing without applying social meanings; the object does not stand for something within real life and social experience is not represented in some way. Children may pour water merely for the enjoyment of watching it flow and the reflection it makes, or they may bury themselves under cushions as a way of experiencing a sense of bodily envelopment and muscular feedback, or they may burn a piece of paper in a flame (if they are allowed!) to watch it change colour and gradually disappear. What they are *not* doing, however, is experiencing themselves and others as social beings in the play, with roles, relationships and socially shareable feelings.

Sensory play can be an extremely rich experience for children, providing powerfully emotional experiences of sight, sound, smell, texture, taste and sense of one's own body in space. Emotions experienced can be frightening and unpleasant or intensely pleasurable, so that children withdraw from or seek out further similar experiences. Sensory play may be carried out in a combined way with other types of play – for example, the visual excitement of watching a pop-up toy appear combined with an imaginary narrative of going to sleep and waking up, or of hiding and being found.

An object may be used in sensory play that is also used in other types of play, but the child's experience of the object will differ. For example, a marble run may be experienced in terms of its 'flow' movement rather than its construction, or a cup for its curved shape rather than as a piece of everyday equipment used for an imaginary purpose. As with other types of play, sensory play is hard to 'see' and an adult may not read the child's experience of play correctly, interpreting what the child is doing with an object as some form of pretence perhaps, or a behaviour that the adult wants to see in the child. Sensory play is an overlooked form of play that is generally viewed by adults as of little or no cognitive relevance or purpose, though adults too enjoy experience for its sensory pleasure.

2. Physical play

Examples: *running, jumping, creeping, crawling, climbing, pushing, pulling, lifting.*

Physical play, also known as large motor play, dominates what many children do in play, though remains under-researched. This type of play is characterised by energetic activity that significantly raises the heart-rate (Pellegrini, 2011). Young children engage in running, jumping, pushing, lifting and other physical activities for the sheer pleasure of doing these things, either by themselves or in coordinated actions with others. However, because physical play activity is often embedded within pretend play scenarios – for example, in boys' superhero play – adults often overlook the physical aspects of children's play to focus on the pretence.

Pretend play is seen as having more cognitive relevance and is therefore of greater interest to adults, but, as noted earlier, a strong case is emerging that physical play serves an important developmental purpose in the opportunity it provides for motor control, self-regulation, strength-building, endurance and stamina (Pellegrini, 2011; Pellegrini and Smith, 1998). Physical play peaks for children in the early years, but can carry on into the pre-adolescent phase, though is more likely to be subjected to regulatory control at this stage.

The concept of 'dizzy play' may be classified as a type of physical motor play. Though there is sensory experience involved in the bodily experience of dizzy play – for example, where children spin round very fast or swing upside down – the vigorousness of dizzy play means it is more of a physical than sensory experience, though the distinction is certainly a fine one.

3. Rough and tumble

Examples: *tickling, holding, being swung, being spun, tumbling, kicking, playfighting.*

Rough and tumble involves rough play where players try not to injure each other whilst engaging in strong bodily contact. Fathers engage more than mothers in rough and tumble with their young children, and boys carry out this kind of play more than girls, though girls do engage in rough and tumble. Rough and tumble is a social form of play that involves players reading each other's social signals and attuning themselves in terms of mental intention and body movement. It is different in this respect to physical play, which is much less social in purpose (Pellegrini, 2011). Rough and tumble is often viewed with mistrust by adults, particularly those working in schools, who view it as aggressive in nature, hard to manage and a fore-runner to real fights breaking out in the playground. However, rough and tumble is thought to develop body control, emotional regulation and social competence. Research finds that it seldom slips into real fighting except for children who have existing difficulty in terms of language, social skill and self-other awareness (Dunn and Hughes, 2001; Holland, 2003). Children often impose rules around rough and tumble – that it should take place on soft ground or that only certain parts of the body should be touched – and may refuse to continue to play if they deem that play has become 'too rough'.

4. Construction play

Examples: *block play, train tracks, building towers, threading, jigsaws, making dens.*

Construction play concerns manipulating two- and three-dimensional materials for the purpose of building something new. Typically, construction play takes the form of using blocks, such as plastic or wooden bricks, to make structures and shapes, the child piecing items together in particular ways. Examples would include building with Lego® bricks, setting out a train track or road system, using blocks to make a tower, and clicking units together to make a geometric shape. The focus of construction play for the child is often on shape, size and space, with the ways that things fit together, the sides, edges, corners, curves and straight lines of the shapes all being of interest. Construction play is a form of small motor play and is often carried out by children in schools and nurseries, though, again, is mostly overlooked in terms of research. As with other forms of play, construction play can take a combined form and is often used in conjunction with fantasy play or pretend play. Building sand castles and dens could be described as construction play that involves a fantasy element, and 'junk-modelling', where junk items are used to create an item of furniture, a building or a creature, could be described as involving an element of pretence.

5. Rule-based play

Examples: *many traditional playground games, such as tag, hide-and-seek, board games, computer games.*

Many traditional games that continue to be played by children today involve rules that determine how elements of a game should be performed. Rules may dictate the amount of time players have to perform an action, how they should move in a game and where they need to go. Rules may cover the sequence of events, how teams are formed and who is 'It'. They will probably determine how a game is won and what happens to the losing side. Rules in games are often flexible, however, with children deciding on the exact rules before they start playing or arguing over the 'proper way to play a game'. Children often change and adapt rules to suit themselves, taking into account the abilities of the players involved, as well as their own interests, preferences and concerns. Sometimes children transfer rules that apply in one game to the playing of another game in a different setting. This often happens in relation to computer games, where children transpose the landscapes, systems, weaponry and rules that exist in a favourite computer game onto a playground game (see Box 1.2). Board games tend to be less flexible in this respect, having rules that are prescribed and written down for players to follow.

Box 1.2   Digital media culture and children's play

A marked difference in children's everyday lives in recent years has been an increase in the use of new digital technologies, such as computer games, the Internet, YouTube and social networking sites. Research into children's play shows that these technologies have had an impact on play too, with children using digital technologies as resources for play ideas, narratives and identities. In this respect, the role of digital technologies in children's play is no different from children's historical use of media culture. Popular songs, comics, advertisements and stories about famous people have been a source of ideas for children in their play throughout history and part of the 'folklore' of childhood (Burn, 2013). Children reproduce characters, actions, gestures, dialogue and sound effects, and refer to stories, settings and relationships, as a way of enriching their play and for other children to recognize and appreciate. Drawing on media sources that are valued by other children is an important way for individuals to construct positive identities within their group and to share an enjoyable experience of play.

Playing computer games, showing an interest in computer games and using ideas from them in other play contexts are something that boys engage in more than girls, though girls participate in gaming too. It is also something that changes with age, as children get older and are able to access more technology. The significance of game playing for schools is that children often borrow structures from virtual game playing for their real-life games with other children. Computer games provide ideas about what actions to perform, how player power is defined and what determines the outcome in a game – for example, how a player is killed or how they might win, and what challenges they must overcome. Children also use their knowledge of computer games to create characters, dialogue, roles and the setting or play world in which they exist. Children try to adapt ideas from computer games to playing in a playground, establishing an understanding between themselves about how something that occurs virtually can be replicated in the here and now. The ways in which ideas from computer games are remembered and reproduced, along with knowledge of the details of games – characters' names, specific pieces of dialogue, the way in which equipment works – are all points of appreciation for children. Very often, children will not actually have experienced playing a computer game, having only heard about it from others or seen it in related media forms, such as posters, captions, dolls or adverts. Knowledge is therefore a key feature of playing, and sharing ideas about a game is something in which all children are usually invested.

Play based on digital technologies often provides a good example of a combined form of play, where imaginative features and pretend actions are present alongside physical play and rough and tumble, children running around, jumping out on each other and carrying out playfighting as part of the pretence. Computer-based play also provides an example of play that does not involve equal interactive turns between players. Games that involve players acting out a narrative and using ideas taken from elsewhere often depend on one child taking the lead in play and directing what others should do.

For some children with autism, gaming and knowledge of computer games are a significant part of their play experience, and something about which they have good knowledge and a great interest. Activities that involve computers and other forms of technology are thought to be particularly suited to the leisure pursuits of autistic people since they involve social worlds that are more predictable, straightforward and manageable for someone with autism (Jackson, 2002). Computer games are highly visual, and often have much clearer rules and outcomes than real-life experiences. Children and young people with autism can be especially good at remembering the small details of a game; they might be able to mimic a character's dialogue with a high degree of precision, and make models of equipment or weaponry with accuracy, all of which are capacities that have value in children's play worlds. Being able to direct other children in play that is based on digital media may be a feature of interaction for an autistic child and their peers. The enjoyment of playing would then depend on the level of knowledge of other children about the digital media source and whether they are happy to follow another player's instructions.

6. Risk taking

Examples: *rope swings, jumping from on high, climbing, sliding down.*

Play is traditionally concerned with seeking out and mastering challenge, pushing boundaries and exploring limits. Risky play is something that children and adults may seek to engage in, but it is usually strictly controlled for children because of the dangers involved. Play spaces are often designed to be as risk-free as possible, and children who want to engage in risk taking usually have to find spaces to play away from adult surveillance. This serves to illustrate the tension that exists in children's play around what children know is acceptable to adults in play and can be played freely and what they know is unacceptable and must be kept hidden from adults. Children understand that play is subject to adult control and can result in discipline and punishment. For this reason, they are often careful about what adults see and may stop playing when observed by an adult, or be evasive in their answers to adult questioning. For adults, therefore, who want to find out about children's experience of play in everyday life, the way in which they ask questions and the quality of their relationships with children are important determinants in how children choose to respond.

7. Competitive play

Examples: *running races, being the first to finish, ball games, making collections.*

An important way in which children construct their social identities is by pointing out distinguishing features about themselves and each other. Who is older, faster, bigger or better at doing something are common concerns that children explore collectively in their play and interactions. Children's games can be competitive where they publicly demonstrate who is the best or fastest at doing something. Children may make drawings and then ask others to judge which is the best, or they may have 'run-offs' to establish who is the overall 'best' within a class, peer or year group. However, being competitive is treated with a degree of caution and ambivalence in children's social worlds. For children, the priority is usually to maintain a state of play with others, and too much competition and ill feeling around winners and losers can get in the way of the continuation of play (Kalliala, 2006). Children often take steps to reduce the level of competition within a game – for example, by giving one player extra 'power', or conversely a 'handicap', or by making allowances and exceptions. Children will often find a way of playing that includes those of different abilities as a way of ensuring that a game is not overly disrupted by players arguing with each other or walking out. They may also counteract competition by introducing an element of chance over who is picked or who has won – for example, by dipping or drawing lots.

8. Language play

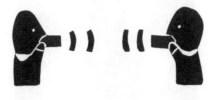

Examples: *stories, rhymes, riddles, jokes, taunts, gibberish, playing with words.*

Language play is associated with verbal competency and mastery in creating certain forms of words. One child may be competent at creating narratives, for example, or remembering the details of a narrative, and so be the player who determines what is acted out in fantasy play. Verbal competency is also demonstrated through the recitation of rhymes, verses, jokes, riddles and raps. A child who is able to memorise and 'perform' these will be viewed by other children with admiration, and a child who is able to create their own will be admired all the more. Language play is sometimes present in the jeers, taunts and teasing comments children make to each other, a child's ability to think of a good 'comeback' also being an important consideration. Language play can involve a preoccupation with word sounds, alliteration and rhyme. Children enjoy creating gibberish language, made-up 'foreign language' and made-up names for things, remembering each other's with pleasure and seeking to create more and funnier ideas.

9. Play using the arts

Examples: *dancing, singing, clapping games, putting on a show, drawing.*

Children often integrate art forms into their play, using dance, music, performance and drawing within their play routines. Using the arts in play is something that is traditionally associated with girls' play – for example, girls performing songs and synchronised dance moves that are adapted from popular culture, engaging in clapping games and other types of musical play, and carrying out art and craft activities. Using the arts in play is linked to the transmission of games, songs, rituals and beliefs, which is part of the traditional practice of childhood, and this occurs from child to child as well as regionally, nationally and historically. Playing with the arts often overlaps with physical play in the form of coordinated movement and dance steps, but also with language play, rule-based play and pretence.

10. Pretend play

Examples: *doll play, small-world play, dramatic role play, superhero play, fantasy play.*

There has been intense academic and educational focus on pretend play, which is viewed by adults as the most important form of play in terms of child development. The onset of pretence has been seen to relate to stages of intellectual growth in the individual, though recent research into early pretence has shown that the child's capacity for pretence is more to do with their social interactions with their carers (Lillard, 2006). It is now understood that pretend play is social in origin and the most sophisticated form of play in terms of social communication. When a child is very young, initial pretend acts are carried out by their carers, who create the child's first symbols, which the child then appropriates as their own (Tomasello et al., 1999). In early pretend situations, the carer engages in complex forms of verbal and non-verbal communication, signalling to the child that 'this is pretence' through exaggerated looking, larger gestures, amplified smiles, repeated actions and the use of a louder and more sing-song voice. The young child brings their own increasingly sophisticated skills to pretend situations too, attending more closely and making greater use of social referencing by looking more at the face of their carer to identify their emotional expression. In situations of early pretend play, social referencing supports the child's understanding of what an interaction means and whether it is 'real' or 'not real'.

In later pretend play, where children play with other children, players continue to engage in high levels of social communication. They strive to achieve a shared intentionality in play, carrying out actions with shared goals by attending closely to each other's communication, body orientation, social cues and emotional expression. Players may not always be successful in this, and the experience of pretend play can be an unsatisfying one, but where good communication and social attunement are achieved, the play will be experienced as highly enjoyable.

Pretend play can be carried out as a solitary act or with another person, but it always relates to the real world. The child's life experiences, personal relationships and knowledge of everyday cultural practices and of emotionally significant events will together provide material for pretend play. But pretend play is a good illustration of the fact that 'what is social' does not exist only as the child's personal experience of routines, roles and relationships. It should also be defined in terms of the wider sociocultural world, with the stories, characters, objects, practices and geographies that exist in books, films, TV programmes, computer games and other forms of media also providing important symbolic resources for the child to draw on, especially as they get older.

Reflective task

Consider the way in which non-autistic people automatically bring social meaning to their perceptions by applying ideas and concepts taken from the sociocultural world. Free-associate on the image of a circle, asking the question, 'What is it?' (e.g. Frisbee, the sun, wholeness). Generate as many ideas as you can. Ask a follow-up question: 'What does this shape represent in your past?'

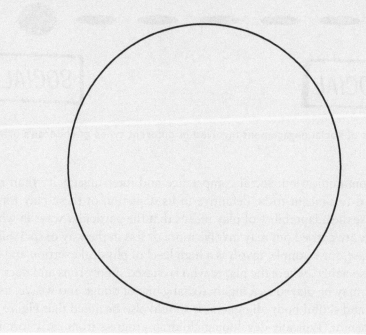

Social versus 'non-social' play

When thinking about types of play that exist for children, it is apparent that different levels of sociability, interactive skill and social communication are present. In Figure 1.1, different types of play have been plotted on a line according to the degree of social involvement. This illustrates the fact that some forms of play, such as sensory play and physical play, require less in the way of social orientation,

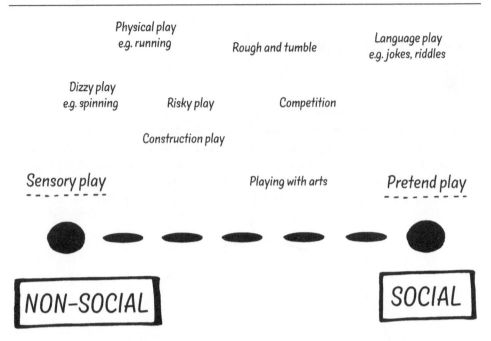

Figure 1.1 Levels of social engagement involved in different types of children's play

interpersonal communication, social competence and intersubjectivity than others. Figure 1.1 is not meant to be definitive in its depiction of these play forms, however, because the adaptability of play means that the particular ways in which these play forms are carried out may involve more or less in the way of sociability. The game of chase, for example, involves a high level of physical exertion and can be played 'non-sociably', where the player who is chased simply runs and does not look back, or it may be played as a highly social game of dodge and weave, using checking looks and skilful body alignment. It should also be noted that Figure 1.1 is not developmental. Typically developing children progress from early forms of sensorimotor play to later capacities in pretence, but they are highly social from the outset. We know that in the neurotypical case the foetus is socially attuned in utero and that from birth the neonate seeks out self-other experiences.

The idea of social versus 'non-social' play, as depicted in Figure 1.1, is useful when we come to consider children with autism and their play. Research indicates that autistic children have preferences in play and are likely to carry out some types of play more than others. Sensory play, physical play and rough and tumble are all preferred forms of play that autistic children continue to engage in beyond the usual cut-off age, whilst difficulty with pretend play is a characteristic feature of autism, though difficulties with other forms of play exist too.

In Figure 1.1, it is possible to see that the play of autistic children features more as 'non-social' play or play that requires less in terms of social competence and interactive skill. However, caution is needed about applying too readily the play experience of neurotypical children to that of autistic children. Autism means a different subjective experience of the world, one that is more sensorily and perceptually based and results in a different cognitive profile. It is probably the case that the experience of play for an autistic child is slightly different for each type of play. Even sensory play for neurotypical children will involve an experience of a social self – '*my* toes dabbling in *my* paddling pool in *my* back garden' – and will not have the sensory absorption of self that some autistic writers describe as their experience. The concept of 'social play' often has quite a specific meaning in relation to children's play – that is, play involving another person. However, in thinking about autism, the understanding of 'social' needs to be understood more broadly: as descriptive of the internal disposition of the typically developing child in play, and therefore fundamentally descriptive of *all* play for non-autistic children, even including their solitary play.

Some issues in relation to play

Play is often conceptualized as something that is universal and good, but research shows that difficult issues exist in relation to play.

Children's right to play

Woodhead (2005) has noted that the current agenda of children's rights in relation to different aspects of their lives gives rise to a tension between children's right to play and their right to development. A central principle of the UN Convention of the Rights of the Child is that play should be recognized as an important feature of children's lives and something they have a right to do. However, children are also viewed as having a right to develop and to be supported and guided in this by their carers and teachers. This sets up a conflict between children's freedom in play and right to control their play and the notion of 'educational play', a context where adults influence and guide children in their play. Educational play concerns the idea of adults designing play spaces for children, selecting play materials and encouraging certain types of play, whilst possibly discouraging others.

Woodhead argues that the issue of play and children's rights requires careful balancing of conflicting issues. He puts forward the idea that adults must take a reflective stance on children's play, assessing what is in children's best interests, respecting the diversity that exists within different childhoods and examining their own values and priorities about play and development. Educational practitioners and parents also need to reflect on what they understand to be child development, particularly in relation to the idea of a 'developmental norm' that may or may not be appropriate for the children in their care.

Play and diversity

Related to this is the fact that though play is universal, it is also extremely diverse and reflects the differences between children and the diversity of different childhoods. Not all children play in the same way, and there are different cultural understandings of what play is. Some children are especially playful and some are more skilful as players. Sutton-Smith (1997) uses the idea of 'low players' and 'high players' to describe differences in motivation and skill that exist between children in play. Children differ in how much play they carry out and what types of play they engage in. Some children are especially imaginative and carry out large amounts of pretend play, whilst others prefer construction or physical play and engage in imaginative play in only minimal ways. The play preferences of some children may be overlooked by adults or seen as not 'real playing'. This could be said of autistic children who play in differential, strongly sensory ways that are not well understood.

Play as a context for social exclusion

Play is often held up as something 'good', but it is apparent to those of us who witness children's play that it can be used as a context for excluding some children. Children's games can be used to reinforce dominant roles that already exist within a peer group and as a context for one child to exert power over others. Some games depend on one child being a leader, and this role can be taken on by individuals with more or less attention to the needs and interests of other players. Woolley et al. (2005) found this is particularly the case for disabled children, whose exclusion from social groups may be reinforced through play – for example, by being given the role of a monster or the 'baddie' in a game.

Chapter 2

Playfulness and children's perspectives on play and friendship

---

Focus of this chapter:

- the difference between play and playfulness
- the play cycle as a framework for reflecting on the experience of play from the point of view of the player
- ethnography as an important method for investigating children's unique play cultures in different settings.

Introduction

We have seen that children's play takes many different forms and can be carried out in highly diverse ways. When we think about what play means we need to consider the wide range of actions and interactions that children carry out in play. Much of what we look at in children's interactions with each other and the environment involves a playful stance and sense of fun, and would constitute a form of play. It would be impossible to list everything children do when they play since it exists in a multitude forms. Part of what children do in play is create new games, novel ways of interacting and entertaining play ideas. However, in order to help us think about what constitutes play for children, Box 2.1 provides examples of some of the different ways in which children play and playfully interact with each other in the setting of a school.

Box 2.1 Examples of children's play and playful interactions

Friends play with hula hoops, seeing how many times they can circle the hoop round their waist and performing a song whilst doing this.

A large group of children run races, using the lines of the playground as start and finish lines and one child acting as starting referee.

A group of friends do karate moves during a creative movement task in a PE lesson, laughing but trying not to let the teacher see what they are doing.

Three children run around the playground, pretending to be horses. They pretend they are a 'horse family' with a designated area as a home and one child narrating the story of what happens.

One boy makes robot hand signals to friends during lining-up time, pretending that he is communicating over a distance and making other children laugh.

One girl slides down the handrail of a set of stairs.

Boys swap football cards and talk about the visual detail and written information on individual cards, discussing which cards are most valuable.

Friends sit at a table, drawing and doing art and craft whilst chatting.

Children make up funny names for each other, using the initial letters of their names.

A group of girls and boys act out scenes from a popular television programme, mimicking plotlines, dialogue, catchphrases and ways of interacting.

Two children play a board game.

Three girls do cartwheels and handstands against one wall of the playground.

Three children pretend to make a potion, using found items in the playground, such as leaves, twigs, conkers and mud.

A group of children compare hand sizes by laying palms together, finding whose is the biggest.

Boys dig holes in the ground to look for treasure.

A group of friends walk along an adventure trail, stepping on logs, swing bridges, beams and stepping stones, following each other in a line.

A small group of friends use a gap in the fence as a door into another world, adopting ideas from a favourite computer game to define what the world looks like and what happens there.

One child races a friend to the top of a climbing frame.

Three children make each other laugh by changing the tag line of a well-known consumer item, inserting funny or rude words.

A group of children perform special feats with their bodies, such as feeling no pain or pretending to lose consciousness.

Play and playfulness

Research into play is increasingly concerned with the fact that the outer features of play – the observable acts that children perform in play, as exemplified in Box 2.1 – do not constitute the core feature of play. The myriad external acts that children carry out in play are being seen by some play theorists as of less significance than *the internal state of mind of the child* as they do these things. This is what is sometimes described as playfulness, or the inner experience of play. Playfulness could be described as the common denominator that underpins children's many play behaviours and the state that determines whether the experience is a playful one.

Sluss (2014) draws a distinction between play and playfulness, noting that they do not refer to exactly the same thing. Play involves external behaviours that can be recognized by someone who is watching the play – for example, a child bringing a cup to the lips as if to drink from it or build a tower in order to knock it down. Playfulness, by contrast, does not involve behaviour that is observable in this way since it concerns the internal disposition of play. Playfulness is characterised by particular internal states, such as spontaneity, creativity, emotional expressiveness and a feeling of personal investment. Importantly, a playful state of mind is one that is experiencing positive feelings of enjoyment, fun, confidence and a sense of well-being. It is an optimum state that involves an intrinsic motivation to engage and experience of flow, or total personal involvement in the activity that is being carried out (Csikszentmihalyi, 1992/2002).

The fact that playfulness cannot be directly observed probably helps to explain why it has been overlooked in research into play. Investigation into children's inner experiences of play is more difficult than investigation of play behaviours, but it is increasingly being seen as a critical context for research and a way of uncovering purpose, form and meaning in relation to children's play. Playfulness has been framed in a number of ways, some of which are outlined ahead.

Measures of playfulness

A variety of measures of playfulness are used within children's services to ascertain the quality of the child's engagement with their learning and their overall emotional well-being, particularly for children in the early years. These measures focus on the child's attitude in the play activity, their emotional responses, the length of time they are engaged and the ease with which they do something. It is often these indices that are seen as best suited to assessing young children's involvement in learning contexts, their acquisition of new learning, their emotional health and well-being and their social development.

Leuven's Involvement and Well-Being Scales

A measure of playfulness that is used in early years educational settings is Leuven's Involvement and Well-Being Scales (Bertram and Pascal, 2002). This is a tool that measures quality of early years settings by looking at children's emotional well-being, self-confidence, self-esteem, resilience and capacity to be involved. It is these areas that are viewed as linked to overall good mental health in the child

Table 2.1 Leuven's Involvement Scale (adapted from Bertram and Pascal, 2002) and Well-being Levels (as developed by Ferre Laevers, 1998)

Child Involvement Scale		Well-Being Levels	
Low activity	Stereotypic, repetitive activity carried out with low energy	**Extremely low**	Child shows extreme signs of discomfort – e.g. cries, looks sad or frightened, bangs head, avoids contact
Interrupted activity	Half of time child engaged in activity includes moments of non-activity – e.g. when child stares into space	**Low**	Posture, facial expression and actions indicate that child is ill at ease
Continuous activity	Child is busy in activity, but energy is lacking and child can be easily distracted	**Moderate**	Neutral posture with facial expression and posture showing little expression
Intense moments	Moments of concentration, energy and persistence; not easily distracted by other stimuli	**High**	Child shows obvious signs of satisfaction, though these signals are not constant
Sustained intense activity	Child shows continuous and intense activity, which can be observed as persistent, energetic and creative	**Extremely high**	Child looks happy, expressive, relaxed and lively; smiles, talks to self and appears confident

and the capacity for 'deep learning' that underpins learning progress and healthy development. Within these scales, the child's degree of involvement is signalled by the energy, concentration, creativity, persistence and precision with which they carry out an activity, as well as how able they are to describe what they are doing and the satisfaction and enjoyment they derive. Table 2.1 sets out categories of involvement and well-being that are identified in these scales.

Test of Playfulness

The Test of Playfulness (Bundy, 1997) was developed within occupational therapy and is perhaps more widely known in health settings. It is an assessment that contains up to 31 items of playfulness in different versions of the test. As with Leuven's Involvement and Well-Being Scales, items are scored following short observations of the child's free play, the child assessed in terms of the intensity and skilfulness of their play, and the proportion of time they spend on a range of

Table 2.2 Sample items in the Test of Playfulness (Bundy, 1997)

Item	Description
Is actively engaged	• Proportion of time spent on activity • Degree to which child is concentrating
Demonstrates exuberance and joy	• Proportion of time child exhibits outward signs of enjoyment
Tries to overcome difficulties	• Degree to which child perseveres to overcome obstacles in order to continue the activity
Modifies activity to maintain challenge or fun	• Ease with which child modifies activity to increase challenge or degree of novelty
Engages in playful mischief	• Adeptness with which child carries out teasing or mischief
Pretends	• Proportion of time child pretends roles, actions, events and objects, and how convincing this is
Incorporates objects and other people in creative ways	• Creativity with which child uses non-toy items and number of different uses found for toy items
Engages in social play	• Proportion of time child interacts with others who are engaged in same or similar activity
Supports play of others	• Ease with which child encourages or scaffolds play of others
Enters a group	• Ease with which child does something to become part of a group already engaged in an activity
Gives clear understandable cues	• Proportion of time child acts in way that gives out clear messages about how others should interact with him/her
Responds to others' cues to further play	• Proportion of time child acts in accord with others' play cues

play activities. Table 2.2 sets out some of the items that are used within the Test of Playfulness.

Children's perception of what is play

Howard (2002) has looked at the issue of the inner experience of play for children by carrying out experimental research into what children perceive as play. She has developed a research procedure for investigating situations that children perceive as 'like play' and 'not like play'. This requires them to sort photographs of classroom activities taken from their own everyday experience. Howard found that children use criteria such as where an activity takes place, what emotion is involved and whether an adult is present to decide what is play. In writing about the essence of play, Howard and McInnes (2013) note that children recognize 'like play' activities because they occur on the floor and within a group of children. No adults are present who are controlling the activity or evaluating children's performance within it, and children expect to experience a positive emotional state. Children perceive activities as 'not like play' if they occur at a table, are more solitary and less associated with positive feelings, and involve an adult controlling the activity and evaluating what children do.

Reflective task

Describe play preferences of children you know. What does play mean for them? When do they seem most engaged and happiest in their play?

Describe your play preferences when you were a child. Remember instances of play when you thoroughly enjoyed yourself. What were you and any play partners doing and what did you find so enjoyable about the play?

The play cycle

When observing play and interaction, it is apparent that the way in which individuals are internally motivated to engage and then cease to be engaged is cyclical in nature. For children, it is possible to see them becoming interested in playing, either with something or with someone, and then to become absorbed and entertained by their play. Eventually, the play episode will end and the child will move on to another activity. As a way of describing how play episodes begin and end and what motivates someone to play, Sturrock and Else (1998/2005) have developed a framework known as 'the play cycle'. The play cycle describes points at which a play episode is initiated and concluded, as well as the actions and responses of the players, all from the players' points of view. Figure 2.1 illustrates key moments of perception for players in the cyclical process of play, from the play cue or initiation of play to the unfolding process of engagement of the players and the ending of the play.

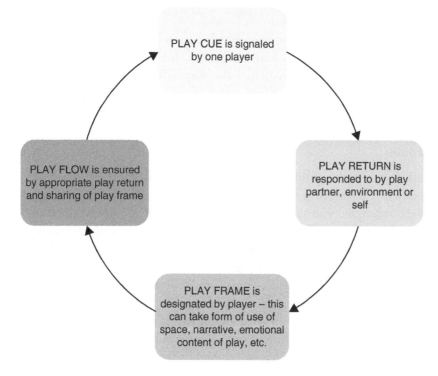

Figure 2.1 The play cycle as devised by Sturrock and Else (1998/2005)

Play cue

The play cue is an action that constitutes an invitation to play. It is something that may be offered by a child or an adult, or by a feature within the environment. Play cues are generally a communication of feeling or thought and can take many forms, but are often very subtle. An expression of the face, such as a smile and knowing look, a playful gesture, a body posture or the presentation of an object may all make up a play cue. The action might take place within the environment, such as the sound an object makes when it falls or the way it responds to touch. A play cue can simply be a verbal invitation to play – 'Will you play with me?' – but this may be too unsubtle and exposing as a gesture since it allows the invitee to be rebuffed with an emphatic 'No, go away!' Play cues can take place as self-experience in the way someone notices something that has happened within their sensory-perceptual experience – for example, the way their body responds or something that comes into view.

Play return

The way in which the play cue is responded to is identified as the 'play return'. The response may come from another person, from the environment or from a person's body, and will signal whether the play will continue or cease. Again, the play return is subtle and often fleeting and constitutes further communication to which the first player must decide how to respond.

Play frame

The play frame is the child's attempt to generate meaning and coordinate the play activity. It concerns a setting out of boundaries within which the play will take place and again can take many different forms. A child may set out furniture or equipment, for example, or outline a narrative or dramatic scene. A play frame may concern an emotional dilemma that is recognizable to other players. Play frames are culturally based and differ across different societies and cultures. Common frames found in children's play in Western societies include dilemmas of being lost and then found, of escaping from danger and of needing to fight. Emotional frames may also concern care and affection themes, such as those that underpin playing games of families and mummies and daddies. In shared activity, the play frame should be recognizable to other players, who participate in it using their cultural knowledge of what is being framed. It dictates up to a point what will happen in the play – players employing existing knowledge and understandings – but it is also subject to change as the play progresses and players add new ideas. Importantly, play is an emergent process that references the wider world, but also involves players' distinctive interpretations of what is being referenced as well as their own personal concerns. Children reproduce these as part of the process of play and as a way of creating their own unique play cultures.

Play flow

Play flow occurs when players are fully involved in the play frame and experience the positive emotions that are associated with playfulness – namely, enjoyment, a sense of fun, confidence and a sense of well-being. Play flow describes the attentiveness and motivation with which people engage in a pleasurable activity. It is an experience that may occur for a very short period of time, perhaps seconds, or for much longer. Sometimes children return to a favourite game over days, weeks, months and even years, experiencing continuous play flow and a heightened state of enjoyment across these time periods.

The play cycle also involves disruptive moments, where the play is interrupted and brought to an end. For those of us working with children with autism, moments of disruption are of interest. Moments where play cues are not responded to or an experience of play flow does not occur will be familiar ones. Two key moments are as follows.

Adulteration

Adulteration refers to the ways in which adults engage in children's play that are experienced by children as 'not play'. These include actions or comments that seek to control the content or form of the play, negotiate between players, 'rescue' one player within a game or use the play as a form of education. These actions are immediately recognizable to children and may cause the play to come to an end and a sense of playfulness to no longer exist. The presence of adults, however, does not always mean that adulteration will occur. How an adult is perceived by children in play depends on how they conduct themselves. Children can perceive adults as true play partners if the adult fulfils the role of another player – that is, someone who recognizes the play frame as set out and engages in it with energy, creativity and enthusiasm.

Dysplay

Dysplay refers to the lack of an appropriate response to a play cue or play frame that prevents the play from advancing. A play cue may be responded to weakly or in a delayed way that means it is missed by the player who signalled the cue. Equally, a play frame may not be recognized by another player as a reference to an aspect of culture that is being appropriated for the purpose of the game. Figure 2.2 illustrates the points at which the play cycle can be disrupted and so come to a premature end.

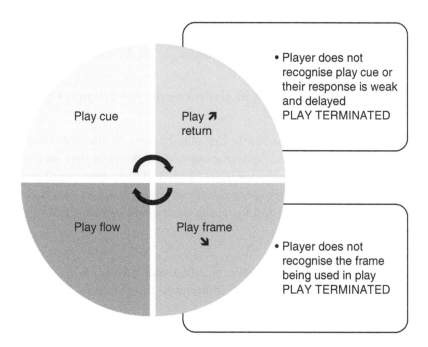

Figure 2.2 A disrupted play cycle, showing points at which play is terminated

Box 2.2 Examples of play cycles

Example 1 describes an episode of rough play, where one player's energetic and aggressive play cue is responded to by another player in an equally energetic way.

Tom swings a large stick around violently as he stands near a group of boys. The stick nearly misses one boy, Lee (PLAY CUE), who looks startled but then smiles briefly and looks at Tom (PLAY RETURN). Tom continues to swing the stick, now aiming it more towards Lee, who tries to catch it each time. Tom tries to swing it near but not too near Lee (PLAY FRAME/FLOW). Lee eventually succeeds in taking hold of the stick and turns the game into a tug of war, the two boys tugging strongly on each end of the stick, trying to wrench it out of each other's hand (PLAY FRAME/FLOW).

Example 2 describes an episode of play where the play return is signalled by the child's body and what it can do.

As Rafiq walks down the school corridor, he starts to make squelching noises with his mouth (PLAY CUE). He experiments with these for a while and discovers that he can make a particularly wet-sounding squelch (PLAY RETURN). He continues to make this sound as he walks, taking steps now in rhythm with the squelching noise, as if he is an alien or monster (PLAY FRAME). He walks in this way the full length of the corridor, stepping carefully and rhythmically with great concentration (PLAY FLOW).

Example 3 describes an episode of play where the play return is signalled by the child's environment.

Seren is putting her toys back into her play basket. As she does this, some shiny beads fall (PLAY CUE), spraying out and sparkling as they hit the floor (PLAY RETURN). Seren looks for more beads and then drops another handful, watching intently as they spray out (PLAY FRAME). She does this again and again, dropping beads and watching them sparkle (PLAY FLOW) until there are no beads left.

Example 4 describes play between an adult and a child, where the adult responds to the play cue but then 'adulterates' the play flow by evaluating the child's performance.

Harry and his dad play a computer game (PLAY CUE/RETURN) that involves fighting and killing zombies (PLAY FRAME). Both players play with excitement, grinning as they see a zombie and letting out groans when one is killed in a gory way (PLAY FLOW). One killing involves a zombie's head exploding in a particularly bloody way and Harry's dad comments critically to Harry, 'I'm not sure you should be playing this game. What certificate is it anyway?' (ADULTERATION).

Children's perspectives on play and friendship

The play cycle highlights the fact that play is *framed* by a player, who sets out a way of playing or play theme that is recognizable to other players. In the play scenarios provided in Box 2.2, play is framed according to the following: one person challenging another to a contest of strength (Example 1), monster-like noises (Example 2), flow of movement (Example 3) and fighting and killing (Example 4). It is apparent from these examples that the way in which play is framed draws heavily on aspects of culture – that is, patterns of behaviour and interaction that exist for and are shared amongst a group of people within a society. It is perhaps only in Example 3 that the play frame does not clearly relate to social behaviour, though even in this instance, there may be some social-emotional expression here too.

Attention to the many ways in which children create play frames helps us to see that their play refers strongly to the sociocultural world of which they are part. More specifically, it tells us something about the specific cultural knowledge a child has and what sense they are making of it. It might also give us insight into what concerns them and how they see themselves or how they want others to see them. Children tap into the cultural information that flows through their social worlds and use it to support their play outlook. However, a challenge exists for those of us seeking to support children in knowing how to attend to this aspect of play. Children's participation in socioculture, like adults', is fast-moving, often subtle and difficult to see. This makes it hard for adults to know the exact social and cultural influences that are operating for a child or group of children at any one time.

Ethnography is widely viewed as the method that is best suited to investigating children's use of culture, including in their play. Ethnographic study involves time spent watching people as they go about their ordinary daily routines, trying to make sense of how their behaviour relates to the contexts in which it occurs. It seeks to reveal the culture that underpins behaviour by paying close attention to its fine details and so 'see' the ideas, practices, beliefs and values that are being drawn upon. Ethnographers study the way in which language and communication are being used by individuals since this also reveals the ways in which they are perceiving and experiencing the world, and negotiating their experiences with those of other people.

It makes sense to see ethnographic-type methods as an important approach to knowing more about children's inner experience of play and the perspective they are taking within play scenarios. Ethnography does not make it possible to know *exactly* what this is, and a level of interpretation will always be necessary. Analysing small units of naturally occurring behaviour, however, is the best way of capturing the ways in which children are internally framing their personal experience, what interests them and what meanings they are making. As Daniels (2008) points out, the study of individual cognition is intimately involved with the study of culture and gives rise to the idea of 'cognitive ethnography'.

The ethnographic work of Allison James over the last two decades (1993, 2013; James et al., 1998) has helped to reframe our understanding of what children do when they interact. Along with other theorists working within childhood studies, James has tried to move research towards more empathetic scholarship and away from a preoccupation with the measurement of children's behaviour. This has been the strong focus of developmental psychology, which, as an approach, has tended to view children as 'becomings' and sought to investigate only the capacities that exist within the individual child. By studying children's everyday interactions in naturally occurring environments, and by talking to children themselves, James has tried to achieve a greater understanding of how children *actually* participate in social processes and the ways in which they make sense of cultural contexts. Her work, and that of other ethnographers of childhood, seeks to identify patterns of culture and the cultural knowledge that is available to specific groups of children within a particular time and place, and how individuals choose to use these. In this way, James argues, children's points of view, social interactions and the unfolding nature of their experience are investigated more reliably.

In James's groundbreaking book, *Theorizing Childhood*, which is joint authored with Chris Jenks and Alan Prout, the point is made that children do not view their interactions with people and the environment as a set of separate practices – for example, as social interaction, friendship and play. From children's own point of view, being friends is closely aligned with the enjoyment derived from playing together, and interacting with another person often takes the form of play. What children see themselves as doing in their interactions is *being with others* and, for this purpose, they employ all the social and cultural knowledge they have. The work of James and others shows us clearly that social engagement is not the use of a fixed set of skills, but is much more an ongoing, creative, interactive and performative negotiation of knowledge and practice within rich social processes.

James's work highlights the importance of thinking about children's social engagement as community practice. Children take on roles, perform actions, use phrases and act out ideas and concerns that are recognized and shared by others. Social engagement depends on all parties having knowledge and some understanding of what the child is 'performing' at any one time. For the child, they must be able to use their knowledge and cultural understanding in a way others in the group can understand and appreciate. The ways in which people participate in cultural communities form patterns of practice over time, and this makes it important to study the patterns that exist for children in peer groups who play together. Identification of patterns in relation to preferred forms of play, play themes, the language used, roles adopted, actions carried out, emergence of conflict and references to the wider culture will all be important in investigating children's play worlds. It is attention to these things that gives insight into the experience of play *for this child* and the specific play culture of *this group of children*. The term 'play culture' refers to the specific practices that are present within particular communities. These relate to the wider culture, but are also unique in the way individuals interpret and use the wider culture and create new cultural norms and practices.

What is instructive in James's descriptions of children's experience of social engagement is the way in which interaction patterns are not firmly fixed for children, at least not as much as they are for adults. Children are in the process of learning forms of social participation that are appropriate to 'being a child' in their particular settings. As James notes, their social competencies and knowledge are emergent and not readily testable in more formal situations. The sociometric methods that are sometimes used to construct children's friendship networks, for example, will probably not be adequate in revealing the 'dense web of social relations' and 'series of seemingly inconsequential and commonplace actions and events' that determine the actual experience of friendship (James, 1999: 17). As James points out, children often nominate one child as 'a friend', but are then observed playing with other children. Observing children and asking them informally about their friendships are more effective as an approach to gaining a rich understanding of their actual experience of social relationships, but involve more prolonged engagement with children in their settings. Box 2.3 provides an ethnographic account of the friendship experiences of Kaylee, aged 8, who has autism. This was gained from making observations of Kaylee and her peers in two settings, watching unobtrusively the natural ways in which the children interacted with each other. Time was also spent talking to staff, parents and the children themselves and revealed that, though the children who associated with Kaylee declared themselves friends, the experience of friendship was markedly different in each of the settings.

Box 2.3   Kaylee's friendship experiences in and out of school

Kaylee, aged 8, is part of a small group of girls who play regularly together at school. There are often conflicts in the group, and Kaylee experiences exclusion from the group at times. She is regularly criticized for being bossy and for telling other people what to do. Two girls are especially vocal in their criticism of Kaylee, calling her names and telling other girls that they should exclude her from the group. Kaylee expresses unhappiness about her friendships in school, but teachers find it hard to know what to do since these girls play well together at times.

Outside of school, Kaylee is a member of a local girl guides group. She enjoys participating in this club, is a regular attendee and sometimes goes away for the night on camps. Kaylee has friends in the group whom she sees every week in meetings and with whom she experiences little or no conflict. One girl, Hannah, who has a brother who is also autistic, gets on particularly well with Kaylee. Another girl, Leigh, experiences some language and communication difficulty herself and is very quiet. All the girls share an interest in art and craft, which is something they often do together in the weekly club.

An ethnographic approach to investigating children's social engagement is well-established practice within education, especially within the early years. Early years practitioners are well-versed in making observations, collecting information about children over a period of time, identifying patterns of behaviour and noting differing forms of participation that exist for different children within different groups. The practice is not well known within autism education, however, despite its interest in children's real life social-emotional experiences. Educational approaches to supporting the learning and development of autistic pupils have been more concerned with generalized knowledge and understandings about autism gained outside of particular settings. However, the individualized nature of autism and need to understand specific practices and interactions mean that closer investigation of children's actual experience of play, interaction and friendship is vitally important. The chapters that follow will look more closely at the particular experience of play for children with autism and what carers and professionals can do to investigate and support this.

Chapter 3

Autism and play

Focus of this chapter:

- current understandings about the play of children with autism, including their preference for certain types of play
- theoretical perspectives on the play differences of children with autism, looking in particular at cognitive-individualistic and social-relational perspectives
- a range of approaches used to support the development of play in children with autism, including behavioural and developmental approaches, the use of peer play, the use of the creative arts, and technology-based approaches
- children's play and the inclusion agenda in education.

Introduction

The play characteristics of children with autism are so well known that they have become part of the myth of autism. The image of the male autistic child playing by himself in a repetitive way, lining up cars, apparently unaware of the social world around, is a potent and familiar one. The inability to play 'like other children play' has been seen to be at the heart of what is different about children with autism and a key area of difficulty. Indeed, difficulties with play, particularly in creating pretend scenarios, were once seen to reflect the core difficulty of autism and pinpoint what autism means for someone.

Current understandings about autism and play

Current understandings about the play of children with autism present a slightly different picture. Children with autism do play in ways that are noticeably different to other children and carry out less play, more solitary play and play where they produce fewer ideas. They spend more time looking away from the play space and enjoy certain types of play, such as rough and tumble, running around and sensory play. But we know that children with autism *do play* and do develop in terms of their play. The picture is actually quite a complex one. It is not true, for example, that all children with autism are unable to create pretend play scenarios. Research finds that 20 per cent of children with autism when tested will spontaneously produce pretend play (Baron-Cohen, 1987), and that others can be encouraged to produce more play, including pretence, when they are supported to do so by another person. Children with autism show differential behaviour when engaging in other types of play too, not only in relation to pretend play, but many go on to develop in terms of their play and their play interests.

This chapter will look at recent research into autism and play, but not with the idea of identifying problems with play. Rather, the emphasis will be on identifying the particular ways in which autistic children play and the possible nature of their development in relation to play. Explanations for the differences in play behaviour of children with autism will be outlined and discussed in relation to the medical model of disability and to social theories of development. Finally, a range of approaches to supporting the development of play in children with autism will be described and considered in relation to the core principles of the inclusion agenda in education.

Autistic preferences in play

Research into autism and play tells us that children with autism have distinct preferences in terms of play. Many studies have shown that autistic children spontaneously produce a higher proportion of what is often described as sensorimotor play (see e.g. Holmes and Willoughby, 2005; Libby et al., 1998). This is an umbrella term for a number of categories of play that include sensory play, physical play, rough and tumble and dizzy play. These forms of play include activities such as playing with the physical properties of objects – for example, by spinning them or watching as they reflect light – carrying out physical play, such as running, jumping and climbing, dizzy play as in spinning and twirling, and engaging in playfighting or 'rough play' (see Chapter 1 for fuller descriptions of each of these types of play). It is not only autistic children who enjoy these types of play. Other children do too, and may engage in a high proportion of any of these types of play, though this may be overlooked by adults in their behaviour too.

In one inventive investigation of the play of children with autism by Doody and Mertz (2013), children were observed in the natural setting of a museum where play activities were on display and available to visitors. The autistic children who were observed showed a clear preference for certain types of activities, all of which come into the category of sensory, motor and perceptual play. They showed a strong preference for climbing stairs and looking down from them, for playing with a windmill and at a table with rice spread over it. They also enjoyed rolling a ball down a track and a game of loop-the-loop with a ball, but enjoyed much less the arts and crafts activities that were available and the vegetable market role play area. All the play activities preferred by the autistic children in the study are ones which come into the category of sensory and physical play, with sensory play encompassing playing with the visual affordances of objects and spaces.

Research also tells us that children with autism are not completely fixed in the way they play. Studies have found that autistic children play differently depending on their play partners, sustaining longer periods of play with partners who are not overly directive, who coordinate themselves more to the child in play and who give them more time to produce play and interaction ideas (El-Ghoroury and Romanczyk, 1999; Hutman et al., 2009). Interestingly, some of these studies show that adults who instruct children in play and seek to direct and control what they do actually engage in briefer play episodes and less play (Freeman and Kasari, 2013).

A medicalized view of autism and play: Problems with this as a perspective

The medical model of disability has dominated the way in which we view autism and our thinking about how to support the development of children with autism. This puts forward the idea that autism is an impairment within the individual that results in a 'deficit of skill' and a 'failure' to develop in ways that reflect a normative developmental pathway. The focus of a medicalized view of autism is fully on the individual, who is seen as requiring the support of interventions in order to develop the skills they are lacking. Teaching is promoted in a didactic form – that is, as a one-way transmission of learning, the teacher identifying very small steps in learning a particular 'skill' and supporting the child to acquire these through repeated instruction.

The development of play in children with autism has come strongly within this perspective, play envisaged as a set of skills that children can be taught. According to this view, children can be taught to use objects in play more interactively with other people, to manipulate objects in ways that suggest everyday pretend actions and to create narratives in play which they act out with toys. Play is seen as something that happens 'on the outside', the actions that children perform in play – bringing a toy phone to their ear as if talking on the phone or walking a toy figure across the table as if to go to the shops – constituting the total play experience. There is little sense that play exists as something 'on the inside' too, in children's feelings about their play, investment in the play and enjoyment of the play situation.

Part of the reason for the emphasis on the outer features of play in autism is that these are measurable. It is possible to observe children's play actions and quantify how much of an identified behaviour is present or whether it is present at all. Measuring behaviour is a key aspect of the cognitive-individualistic view of development that exists within autism theory and practice. This is aligned with the medical model of disability and makes a strong link between what children do in their play and their development of cognitive functioning. Within this perspective, Piaget's (1954) idea of developmental stages of intellectual growth is used as a framework to describe the development of play in children with autism too, often to the exclusion of any other ideas about play and what it means. Piaget argued that children move through different stages of play in a way that reflects cognitive development, at first playing with objects in sensorimotor ways that are suggested by their immediate physical properties (i.e. mouthing them, tapping them, throwing them), but then moving on to later stages of functional and pretend play. These involve more and more sophisticated ways of engaging with objects and applying meanings to objects that are not suggested by the child's immediate environment. Piaget put forward the idea that children's intellectual growth comes about in the way they individualistically develop abstract ideas or 'schemas' about objects that are 'decoupled' from here-and-now presentations and relate more to the child's developing knowledge of the wider world. Accordingly, if pretend actions can be quantified in children's play behaviour, then an increase in the number of these is held to be evidence of intellectual growth.

Though Piaget's ideas about play and child development have been very influential and remain relevant in terms of the idea of stages of growth, several problems exist in using this as a single account of what children do in play. Piaget took a narrow view of play, focusing only on certain types of play as cognitively relevant. He put great emphasis on the development of one type of play, pretend play, but gave much less importance to other types of children's play. This is hugely important when thinking about autism since it is these other types of play – sensory play, physical play, rough and tumble, rule-based games, dizzy play – that dominate the play of children with autism. Piaget's linking of individual stages of intellectual growth with particular cognitive abilities is also too simplistic an account of human development. He set out a fairly fixed developmental pathway and argued that this applied to all human beings. We know now that development involves a complex interaction of brain, cognition, behaviour and environment, involving biological and social processes that are highly interrelated. Not all children develop in the same way, and development itself is highly contingent on the child's experiences of interactions with their carers and other sociocultural influences in their environment.

One final point to make here is that the lack of any real consideration of children's internal disposition and emotional experience in play – something that

Piaget did not emphasize – is problematic within perspectives on autism and play. In the previous chapter, we have seen that it is children's inner experience of play that constitutes the essence of play. Children's motivation to engage, attitude in play and positive emotional experience of play are really what determines whether an experience is play. Play in autism is envisaged as having adult-directed goals and involuntary actions on the part of the child with autism, and this must raise the question whether what happens in much of play learning in autism education is really play.

Perspectives on play differences in autism

Explanations for why the play of autistic children is different to that of non-autistic children relate to the perspective that is taken on what autism is as well as the perspective taken on the nature of human development. Within autistic theory and practice, two contrasting perspectives are dominant and are probably best encapsulated in the idea of 'cognitive-individualistic' accounts and 'social-relational' accounts, as described by Hobson et al. (2015). Cognitive-individualistic accounts are sometimes also known as cognitive theories of autism and focus on cognitive impairment within the autistic person. Discrete areas of cognitive functioning, sometimes termed 'cognitive mechanisms', are seen as the basis of any difficulty, and disability is something that 'belongs' to the individual. Cognitive-individualistic accounts have already been mentioned earlier in relation to a medicalized perspective on autism that prioritises a skills-based approach to play development and sees a need for the quantification of children's behaviour in play.

By contrast, social-relational accounts accept the biological basis of autism but view difficulties that exist for people with autism as partly the result of a secondary inability to engage interpersonally within close relationships. Social-relational accounts emphasize the importance of richly experienced and intensely felt experiences of relating to other people, particularly within children's very early interactions with close family members, to the later development of cognition and social understanding. It is from repeated interactions within these very close relationships that the perspective or subjectivity of the other person is taken on as an experience of 'intersubjectivity' (Hobson, 2002). Intersubjective engagement is thought to facilitate deep emotional learning and provide the basis for the development of higher levels of cognitive functioning, ones that involve the individual moving away from perception- or memory-based cognition and towards abstract and complex thought, where different points of view are considered and experience can have several meanings, derived from both self-experience and experience of the other.

Some caution is needed when thinking about these two perspectives on autism and development, however. The complex and interrelated nature of human development means that it is rather artificial and not always helpful to discuss theories of development as if they are unrelated to each other. For example, social-relational accounts accept that autism is biologically based and do not see social relations as causing autism. This is important since a historical explanation for autism was that bad parenting and the failure, particularly of mothers, to show affection to their children caused the condition. Social-relational accounts view the primary impairment of autism as something that someone is born with, and argue that this interferes with learning and development that are essentially socially based. What further complicates the picture is that social-relational accounts are concerned with cognition and also see the development of cognition as the goal of development. Rather confusingly, they could therefore be described as another kind of 'cognitive theory'.

Conversely, recent cognitive theories of autism do generally recognize the importance of children's participation in social engagement with other people to their learning and development and do not exclude the social environment as playing a part in the development of cognitive function. Increasingly within cognitive-individualistic accounts, cognitive development is put forward as the result of the interaction between a person's genes, their brain maturation and their environment, including social engagement with others (Pellicano, 2012). The issue is more one of emphasis and focus, cognitive-individualistic accounts emphasizing development *within the individual* and the focus of support as being the individual child. Social-relational accounts point to the existence of neurodiversity in the human population and see support needing to focus more on environmental adaptation and acceptance of difference.

Cognitive-individualistic perspectives on play differences in autism

Cognitive explanations for differences in the play of autistic children seek to identify cognitive mechanisms within the individual that impede or promote the capacity for play. An early account, put forward by Leslie (1987), used the fact that children with autism experience difficulty in passing theory of mind tests to explain their difficulties with play, specifically their difficulties with pretend play. Leslie made a link between theory of mind, which involves the capacity to represent reality as it exists for someone else, and the child's capacity for pretence. He argued that both theory of mind and pretend play involve 'metarepresentation' or the ability to hold in mind another person's mental reality (see Box 3.1 for a fuller explanation). Leslie thought that the inability to metarepresent explained a child's autism and posited that children with autism were incapable of carrying out pretend play because of their difficulties with metarepresentation.

Box 3.1   Metarepresentation

Alan Leslie argued that engaging in pretend play requires the cognitive skill of 'decoupling' from reality as one perceives it and keeping in mind an alternative reality. He used the example of a child holding a banana to their ear and pretending it is a telephone. Leslie made the link between this decoupling from the reality of a situation that occurs in pretend play and the understanding of people's inner mental states, which are hidden and which are referred to as a child's theory of mind. In order to have theory of mind, it is necessary for the child to hold in mind another person's reality, thereby creating a 'metapresentation' of reality or representation of reality that is different from perceived reality. Leslie argued that both pretend play and understanding people's false beliefs ('theory of mind' as measured, for example, in the Sally and Anne test) involve the capacity for metarepresentation and that this does not 'switch on' when a person has autism.

More recent theories have criticized metarepresentation as too complicated an account for what children do when they pretend. Pretend play does not necessarily involve representing someone else's reality, and is more often simply an imitation of someone else's actions. When young children first start to pretend, moreover, it is within interactions with their parents and carers, where communication is rich and the child fully engaged. Adults use sophisticated forms of social communication to flag up for a child that they are 'pretending', and the child pays special attention to the adult to gain an understanding of what it is they are doing.

Ideas about how children develop a theory of mind have moved away from the notion that it is a capacity that 'switches on' at the age of 3 or 4. What is increasingly seen as of importance to the understanding of other people is the child's social experiences, particularly of close family relationships, and their language abilities and capacity to engage in conversations about hidden mental states (see Hughes, 2011, for an excellent appraisal of current ideas about children's social understanding). Theory of mind is much more a reflective stance that emerges slowly as a child develops and is able to engage in thoughtful consideration of other people's experience. However, even very young children have an understanding of other people's intentions within interactions, which they may not be able to express or be tested on, but can nevertheless respond to.

Problems with Leslie's metarepresentational explanation for autism and autistic differences in play have emerged. Researchers have shown that some children with autism can be supported to carry out pretend play and that any difficulties with play are not the result of an absolute inability to recognize pretence. Research studies carried out by Lewis and Boucher (1988, 1995), Libby et al. (1998) and Jarrold et al. (1994, 1996) all found that children with autism can carry out pretend play if they are supported to do so, especially when they are provided with play ideas. They found that some children with autism produce pretend play spontaneously and without support and postulated that any difficulties with pretend play for children with autism are not therefore a 'competency' issue, or innate inability to carry out pretend play. Any difficulty with play in autism is seen more as an issue of 'performance' – for example, that children experience problems in play because they are unable to generate ideas or 'play schemas'.

In recent years, cognitive theories of autism have looked beyond problems with pretend play and highlighted the fact that autistic children experience difficulties with other types of play too (Williams et al., 2001). There has been increasing interest in executive function difficulty in autism as a possible explanation for the range of differences that are observed in the play of children with autism (Jarrold and Conn, 2011). Executive function is a descriptive term for a number of cognitive functions that support higher-order thinking, including working memory, attentional flexibility, planning and execution within tasks (see Table 3.1). These are important capacities in play – for example, in planning and keeping track of ideas produced in play scenarios as they unfold. In pretend play, there is a requirement for a large number of capacities involving planning, memory and shifting attention, as well as inhibiting the everyday functions of objects in order to assign an imagined alternative.

Executive function as an explanation for difficulties with play gives rise to the idea of addressing 'deficit skills' in children with autism. At its crudest level, this

Table 3.1 A range of executive functions

Planning	The effective planning and execution of a task according to a goal.	**Measured by:** *Tower of London task:* Change the configuration of a set of beads in the smallest number of steps in response to a visual instruction.
Working memory	Holding information in mind whilst performing a task.	*WISC Digit Span test:* Repeat a set of numbers forward and then backward.
Attentional flexibility	Shift the focus of your attention within a task.	*Card-sorting task:* Sort a set of cards according to one rule (e.g. a given shape) and then according to another rule (e.g. colour).
Inhibitory control	Hold a rule in mind and respond appropriately, whilst aware of and resisting another influence.	*Luria's Hand game:* Copy another person's hand movements in the opposite sequence (i.e. resisting the visual influence of what the other person is doing).

may be seen as simply providing intense and repeated experiences of one area of functioning – for example, repeated practice of a play narrative to reinforce the remembering of it. However, more in line with how children develop, an approach to developing executive function may be seen as a matter of supporting skills in joint attention, which require shifting attention, and in verbal communication as a way of mediating cognitive capacity.

Social-relational perspectives on play differences in autism

Social-relational accounts do not make a strong distinction between the cognitive capacities needed for pretend play and those used in other types of play (Hobson et al., 2013). All play is seen as socially based and requiring an ability to participate in communicative interpersonal relationships and make sense of the social world. As we have seen in Chapter 2, even the solitary play of a non-autistic child draws on social understandings and patterns of social interactions, relationships and practices in children's everyday worlds. Pretend play requires the *most* skill in this respect, requiring very high levels of social communication and close alignment of intentions in play with other players. Players adjust themselves mentally to each other and to the meanings that are being assigned to objects and actions used in the play. They do this by paying close attention to each other's communication and social behaviour, and any elaboration of pretend play is also communicated in this way, players continuing to attend to any new ideas that are introduced. Early pretend play encounters between a young child and their carer involves just this kind of rich social communication, where part of the purpose of interaction is to take in fully what the other person is doing, communicating and feeling (Striano et al., 2001) (see Box 3.2).

Social-relational accounts of play differences in autism focus on moment-to-moment interactions between two play partners, particularly interactions in the early play encounters of young children and their carers. This is a way of emphasizing the importance of interpersonal relatedness and shared intention in play. However, as Ochs et al. (2004) point out, autism interferes with learning about the wider social world too and the development of 'dense networks of meaning' about social roles and practices that children also bring to their play. This also interferes with the creation of shared play narratives and recognizing the way in which play invitations are being framed.

Box 3.2   Early pretend (symbolic) play

Pretend play is increasingly being viewed by researchers as something that is social in origin. Young children learn early symbolic acts when supported to do so by adults, performing actions with objects that they first see adults doing

(Striano et al., 2001). In early playful interactions, adults use social behaviours to indicate that something is 'not real'. Research using slowed-down video footage of mother and child interactions shows that mothers signal they are pretending by making exaggerated use of space when performing pretend actions – for example, using larger motor actions to perform 'eating with a spoon'. When they do this they look at the child more than if they were really eating with a spoon, smiling more often at the child too and for longer. In pretence, adults change the quality of their voice, using a sing-song and louder voice, perhaps with an accompanying sound effect. Words and actions used by adults in early pretend play are fewer in number, but performed in a repeated fashion. The child also uses social behaviours in situations of pretend play, looking more and for longer at the person performing the pretence, glancing back and forth between their partner's actions and the expression on their face as a way of understanding their feelings and intentions (Lillard, 2006).

Some social-relational accounts of development see these experiences of pretend play, alongside other early experiences of interaction, as the basis for a later capacity for symbolic thought. For young children, richly experienced social communication with their carers, which is highly repetitious in nature, provides access to other people's minds and ideas over time. In early interactions, face, voice, gesture, gaze and movement are richly used within enjoyable moments of 'intersubjective' engagement. These meaningful moments of social and mental alignment are experienced repeatedly and take on a kind of language of engagement, starting to exist as 'things in themselves' and forming symbols for wider use that relate to the child's social understanding.

 Reflective task

Reflect on personal experiences of intensive relationship-based support work, using play and playful interaction with a child with autism. Describe the following:

- the child's behaviour
- your emotional response to the situation
- how you perceived your role in the relationship

- what you did and said in response to the child
- what you believe was the child's experience of you.

Would you do anything differently given the same situation again? Listen to each other's stories in pairs and small groups of three.

A praxis perspective

A different perspective on autism and play focuses on the bodily nature of play and the way in which children embody and enact ideas in their play. The word 'praxis' refers to the act of embodying, engaging with, applying and practising ideas and could be said to be directly relevant to what children do in their play (Kuhaneck and Britner, 2013). The sensory processing difficulties of autism mean that basic body awareness is experienced differentially, and this is thought by some theorists to interfere with the creative way in which the body is used in play.

A sensory perspective

Rogers et al. (2005) have put forward the idea that autistic children may show more sensory interest because of their underinvolvement in social relationships. Within this perspective, the intense sensory engagement seen in the play of children with autism is viewed not as a primary result of sensory processing differences but as more of a secondary symptom arising from a need to create an alternative form of engagement with the world.

Other sensory-based explanations of play differences in autism focus on the experience of sensory engagement itself for the autistic child. Using a range of measures of play and playfulness in children, Eisele and Howard (2012) found that autistic children's behaviour described as ritualized and repetitive actually fulfils much of the criteria of play, particularly of a playful attitude within activity.

Typical and atypical development

Consideration of the different explanations of autism and play difference provides insight into the different ways in which the development of children with autism is conceptualized. Cognitive-individualistic accounts tend to see development as taking place in a 'typical' way – that is, children with autism developing the same cognitive skills as children without autism given the right kind of intervention or approach. According to these accounts, the key is to isolate cognitive areas that are lacking or underdeveloped and focus on their development, giving a kind of kick-start to development that will then follow a normative pathway. According to this view too, play is conceptualized as an aspect of cognitive functioning that requires development in a similar vein to language, communication and interaction, but as a different or overlapping set of skills.

An alternative view of development in autism is that it is atypical and does not follow a neurotypical pathway. According to this view, the neurological processing differences that are present in autism – that interfere with the ordinary ways in which children develop – result in different cognitive processes and the development of a different kind of brain. Many proponents of a social-relational approach to autism and play argue that the processes involved in ordinary social interaction and play are too complex for children with autism to learn (Hobson, 2011; Ochs et al., 2004). They see autism as a natural form of 'neurodiversity' that is on a par with other neurodevelopmental conditions, such as ADHD or developmental coordination difficulty. In these accounts, it is much more important to recognize and accept difference and to find ways for people to live as they are, rather than be forced into some idea of neurological 'normalcy' that is not realizable in actuality. Inclusive support systems, heightened awareness and understanding by others, assistive technologies and clearer systems of communication are all seen as important forms of environmental adjustments and support.

The idea of atypical development in autism gives rise to the idea that children's play exists atypically too, as a natural expression of a subjective experience that is sensory-based rather than socially mediated. The play we see in children with autism may not be exactly the same as that we see in non-autistic children. Our interpretations of play behaviours may be *seeing* pretence in children's actions, for example, but we are not able to say for sure that these are pretend actions as they are understood within 'typical play'. Or conversely, we may be *seeing* stereotypic behaviours in a child, which we deem 'problematic', but it could be the case that the child's experience is of an enjoyable form of sensory play. By applying an overlay of expectation derived from concepts of typical play, we might be failing to recognize 'atypical play' and losing sight of what is of value to the child.

The next chapter, which outlines personal accounts of the experience of play by autistic writers, explores this issue further. It provides insider descriptions of enjoyable childhood experiences of play that could be said to constitute autistic play cultures, many of which are based in sensory rather than social engagement with objects and the environment. Beforehand, this chapter will outline the range of approaches that are used currently to support the development of play in children with autism and discuss their relevance in relation to inclusive education.

Approaches to supporting the development of play

In many theories of human development, play is seen to perform a key role. For Piaget, children's playful interaction with objects is an exploration of the environment that leads naturally to cognitive growth. For Vygotsky (1978), whose sociocultural theory of human growth emphasized the central importance of interactions with other people, play is behaviour that precedes development. He found that children are particularly engaged when they are playing, showing greater motivation and asserting more self-control, and concluded that play is an optimum learning environment. Children's positive experiences of pleasure, excitement, absorption and creativity in play are seen as having importance alongside the manipulation of objects and performance of play actions. For Vygotsky, children develop through richly experienced interactions, emotional experiences of relationships and the internalization of these. He was interested in the influence of both outer and inner experience on the development of play, and so could be said to have an enriched view of play.

Following on from these theories of child development, the importance of play to the development of a child with autism is often seen as a key feature of theory and practice. However, approaches to supporting the development of play in children with autism, of which there are a large number, differ not only in technique but also in the conceptualization of what constitutes play and the nature of the link between play, learning and development. Some approaches see the outer performance of play – the actions that are performed – as the only criterion of importance, but others take the view that play situations for children with autism are important in terms of the inner experience of play too. Moreover, some theorists and practitioners believe that children's play has 'instrumental value' only in that it has the single purpose of providing a context for learning and development. Others believe that play has both instrumental value and intrinsic value in that it also provides children with an important leisure pursuit and form of entertainment that supports well-being (Goodley and Runswick-Cole, 2010). Theorists and practitioners hold different beliefs about the purpose of what they are doing when they support the development of children's play. This should be kept in mind when considering the different approaches to the development of play in autism that exist. A range of these is outlined ahead with reference made to whether they address the instrumental value of play or both the instrumental and intrinsic value of play.

Behavioural versus developmental approaches

Behavioural approaches are predicated on the idea that learning takes place as a consequence of reinforcements following on from an action. These can be either positive or negative, the former encouraging the ongoing use of a behaviour and the latter its cessation. The aim of a behavioural approach to learning is to target behaviours that have been identified as key to a child's development in a particular area, whether it is communication, language, cognition, social interaction, play or independent living skills. In order for the approach to be implemented, it is important to break down the learning into small incremental stages or teaching steps, each one reinforced and learned before moving on to the next.

Very often, a behavioural approach to developing play in children with autism involves following a developmental progression from early forms of sensorimotor play to later stages in construction, functional and pretend play. Play is seen as having instrumental value, but no intrinsic value as a source of leisure, entertainment or fun. The goal of learning in relation to play is for the child to be able to create pretend scenarios, this being seen as an 'endpoint' in the development of children's play. Other forms of children's play tend not to be seen as a goal of play learning, though children may be encouraged to interact in playful ways with others as part of the skills that are included in communication or social interaction developmental pathways.

A behavioural approach to learning emphasizes the direct transmission of knowledge and skill, the teacher or therapist imparting and reinforcing these and supporting children in rehearsing a skill or piece of information. This stands apart from other theories of learning, notably developmental theories that see the child as actively engaging in and shaping their learning and the learning process itself as a two-way negotiation of teaching and learning. A developmental approach to learning puts forward the idea that children are not passive learners, but participate actively in learning contexts, making sense of learning experiences by bringing their own ideas, interests and concerns. They negotiate these through language and interactions with their carers and teachers to help create the learning experience, producing new learning and moving themselves forward in their understanding. Learning is envisaged not as something 'done to' the child but as something that occurs within the learner, mediated through social interaction, much as Vygotsky envisaged it.

Developmental approaches in relation to play take an integrated view of play and see it as having instrumental value in terms of cognitive growth, but also intrinsic value as emotional expression, social participation and realization of self. Play is seen as needing to involve intrinsic motivation on the part of the child as well as enjoyment of the play situation and of playful relationships. Play development is not something that can be forced or directed by an adult. Rather, the role of the adult is to recognize the child's interests and concerns and engage with these, using them to support or scaffold increasing amounts of social engagement in play as a way of achieving interactive play. Box 3.3 describes two approaches used with autistic children for the purpose of play development. One of these, applied behaviour analysis, is a behavioural approach, and the other, DIR®/Floortime™, is an example of a developmental approach.

Box 3.3   Behavioural versus developmental approaches to play

Behavioural: Applied behaviour analysis (ABA)

The Lovaas model of applied behaviour analysis (ABA) (Lovaas, 2003) is based on the principle of a behavioural approach: that skills can be taught using positive reinforcement. Intensive programmes of support involve a systematic progression through small-step 'treatment goals' based on normative frameworks. Initial assessment is important in measuring the child's level of development and informing an individualized treatment programme to target deficit skill areas. Thereafter, skills are taught as part of a sequence of teaching steps – for example, the development of expressive language involving cooperation with simple requests and imitation of non-verbal actions, increasing vocalization and imitation of sounds, and finally 'chaining' these skills to form words, which are then associated with objects. The ongoing gathering of data on a child's achievements is an important feature of an ABA approach since this is seen as a way of measuring progress and demonstrating development.

Within an ABA treatment programme, children's play is taught as a series of actions that can be prompted, practiced and reinforced. In teaching pretend play, for example, teaching steps may involve modelling everyday actions, such as washing hands, teeth and hair, and then prompting and practising these repeatedly over weeks and months. Eventually, a child is encouraged to carry out a whole scenario of play, combining these actions and acting out an entire scene, such as taking a bath.

ABA is probably the best-known behavioural approach used with autistic children and is the most widely researched. However, a range of other approaches exist, including pivotal response training, where the teacher follows the child's lead in choosing activities and determining how to play with toys, and the Early Start Denver model (Rogers and Dawson, 2010), which is an early intervention programme that applies ABA goals to playful interactions with young children within a relationship-based approach.

Developmental: DIR®/Floortime™ model

The Developmental, Individual-difference, Relationship-based (DIR) model was devised by Stanley Greenspan in response to problems associated with behavioural approaches to autism, specifically the generalization of learned behaviours. DIR/Floortime is a developmental approach that emphasizes the importance of parents joining in with their child's activity as a way of bringing them more into a socially interactive world. The principles of this model reflect the way in which children's development is typically mediated through repeated experiences of interaction within richly enjoyable communicative relationships (Greenspan and Wieder, 2006).

Within this model, play is envisaged as a platform for children's communication, expression, exploration and enjoyment, much as it is for all children. Floortime is the play component of the DIR model and involves the adult understanding and accepting whatever the child is doing, and not imposing an alternative activity. The adult's engagement with the child's interests and activity has the goal of bringing about a shared experience of that activity and thus a social enrichment. The adult must work hard to make sense of children's experience whilst maximizing their enjoyment of any shared engagement and social interaction. Experiences of warmth, rich communication and shared interest within safe and trusting relationships are all important features of the model.

Careful analysis of the developmental capacity of the child and any sensory processing differences they may be experiencing forms part of initial assessment and supports the setting of learning goals. Developmentally informed 'milestones' taken from typical development are used for this purpose, identifying self-regulation and social engagement as early goals, and moving on to higher levels of functioning that relate to thinking and problem solving. Higher levels of functioning are associated with certain forms of play development, specifically the child developing the capacity to carry out pretend or symbolic play. The process of assessment provides the parent or therapist with information about the meaning of children's actions and how to respond appropriately and effectively within Floortime engagement.

There are numerous other developmental approaches that promote playful engagement and shared communication within a naturalistic relationship-based learning environment. An example would be Intensive Interaction (Nind and Hewett, 2005), which aims to provide children with experiences of the communicative interactions that precede speech.

Peer play

Research indicates that children with autism achieve more learning within interactions with peers and siblings than within adult-mediated interactions. This makes approaches to the development of peer play perhaps particularly significant. It is certainly the case that in inclusive education, children playing with other children is of more relevance than adult-child play. However, support for peer or sibling play is challenging since the presence of an adult, especially one who is evaluating what children are doing, usually means that the context is no longer experienced by non-autistic children as one of play. Peer play is an important issue for inclusive education and is discussed at greater length in Chapter 4. Box 3.4 provides two examples of approaches to developing play in children with autism that are based on peer interactions.

Box 3.4   Peer play approaches

Integrated play groups (IPGs)

Integrated play groups were developed by Pamela Wolfberg (1999) to support the development of peer play, including children's play skills, communication and quality of play. IPGs use the idea of 'expert' players, who are non-autistic children, playing and interacting with 'novice' players, who are children with autism. Expert players are peers in a school setting who have good skills in interpersonal communication and play, and siblings in a home setting. Prior to children being invited to play, careful consideration is given to the selection of play materials, the play space and the play preferences of the child with autism. During play sessions, an adult facilitator uses social guidance techniques to support both expert and novice players, suggesting play actions, narrative ideas and things players can say to each other. Suggestions may also concern players' social communication – for example, an expert player being advised to first get the attention of a novice player before carrying out an action in play. In this way, IPGs address the social communication of all players, supporting all children to recognize, interpret and respond appropriately in play. Studies of the efficacy of IPGs report gains in amounts of play engagement, including in pretend play and social interaction skills (Wolfberg et al., 2015).

LEGO®-based therapy

LEGO®-based therapy (LeGoff et al., 2014) harnesses the preference that many children with autism show for construction play to support the development of social interaction. It uses Lego bricks as a medium within play groups to support children's motivation to engage with others and ability to maintain interaction over a period of time. Lego bricks are identified as a particularly enjoyable play medium for children, though other kinds of toys and sets of instructions could equally be used. Groups involve a straightforward and formal arrangement of social roles, with children taking turns to adopt designated roles. Roles include 'the engineer', who provides instructions for building, 'the supplier', who finds the pieces, and 'the builder', who follows instruction and builds the set. A clear set of group rules is provided, which include using verbal communication to negotiate interactions between players. The complexity of groups can develop, from pairs to groups of three or four, with the aim of children eventually being able to build their own creations, using more freestyle interactions.

Creative and therapeutic approaches involving play

The creative arts – for example, music, movement and drama – are used within a range of approaches to developing play and interaction in children with autism. The use of the creative arts is seen as a way of mediating social interactions for autistic people and making them more manageable and enjoyable – for example, drama used to analyse micro-moments of social interaction (Conn, 2007). The creative arts can be used to provide non-threatening, calming and socially accessible forms of communication and interaction, which in turn encourage personal expression, self-awareness, self-regulation and flexibility. When used within groups, the creative arts support awareness of others, social skills and group bonding.

The creative arts can also form part of therapeutic developmental approaches to autism that are relationship-based. These emphasize the importance of rich experiences of relationships to children's development, where the therapist is attuned to the child's needs and communication, understands and accepts the child as they are and provides experiences of warmth and positive regard. Play and the creative arts may be used as a way of bringing this about, the therapist joining the child in their play activity and using creative expression to mediate interactions and produce gentle situations of social sharing.

Box 3.5 Creative and therapeutic approaches involving play

Music therapy

Like other forms of creative arts therapies, there is a need to distinguish the therapeutic use of music to support interaction and communication from a psychodynamic experience of relatedness through the medium of music that is more descriptive of a therapeutic relationship. Music is often used with autistic children to support their expression and experience of communication, with reported effects including a reduction in self-stimulatory behaviours, increased communication and increased ability to follow instruction. The benefits of using music with children with autism are thought to reside in the calming effect of music on brain circuitry and subsequent enhanced capacity for shared attention, the mediation of social interaction via a musical instrument rather than difficult face-to-face interactions, and the provision of an alternative, non-face-to-face, non-verbal form of communication (Berger, 2002; Wimpory and Nash, 1999). Music is used both as a platform for non-threatening interaction and as a support for interaction that takes another form.

Play therapy

There is a range of play therapy approaches to autism, but perhaps the best known is non-directive play therapy. This was developed by Virginia Axline (1964) in the 1960s and is a child-centred approach. In non-directive play therapy, it is the psychodynamic relationship between the child and the therapist that is seen as the primary source of development. Since the potential for growth is seen to depend on change in the way the individual experiences another person within close relationships, it is important that the therapist provides warm and congruent experiences of relationship, accepting the child as they are and trying to understand their point of view. Other forms of play therapy exist which focus on slightly different aspects of caregiving relationships. For example, developmental play therapy (DPT), developed by Viola Brody (1997), emphasizes the importance of touch within relationships, seeing this as a key feature of early infant-caregiver relationships and the basis for development of self-other awareness and a healthy sense of self.

Animal-assisted play therapy

Animal-assisted play therapy emerged out of play therapy sessions where the therapist had an animal in the room, usually a dog, and noted that interactions between the child and the animal were easier, more communicative and more reciprocal than with a human being. Sometimes people with autism report that they find interaction with animals less socially stressful than with humans, some describing closer emotional connectedness and more effective communication. The goals of animal-assisted play therapy are similar to the relationship-based goals of play therapy – for example, positive experiences of communication, heightened social awareness, consideration of another's needs and adjustment to these, and recognizing emotion in another living being (VanFleet and Colţea, 2012). In responding to an animal, there may be more need for a child to self-regulate and assert self-control over their movements and noise, and to give instructions, all experiences of relatedness thought to support good self-esteem and a sense of well-being.

Technology-based approaches to play

Many writers have noted the importance of access to digital technologies for autistic people. Very often, children with autism are more drawn to the television, computer, iPad and interactive whiteboard than they are to people and real-life interactions. When using these technologies, children may be more engaged, focused and able to follow instruction, and may be more able to self-regulate. It is thought that digital technologies provide an interactive environment that is more manageable for them, having reduced and predictable interactions with a highly visual quality and often clear rules. The child may feel they have more control over what is occurring than they experience in real life, with more opportunity to engage in repeated experience that is exactly the same. For some writers, access to computers, technology and the Internet has enabled an autistic community to exist for the first time and a culture of autism to emerge (Singer, 1999).

Children's play and technology have an interesting relationship since, although a strong link clearly exists, it is not one that is necessarily cast in a positive light by adults. Technologies and media culture are a huge influence on what children do in their play, both directly as play media and indirectly as ideas that children use in other forms of play – for example, in games they play in the school playground. Yet, there is very often a tension between the influence of technology- and media-based play in children's lives and the influence of parents and teachers, who may dismiss this type of play as unrefined, unchallenging and educationally irrelevant.

The use of technology-based ways of developing the play of autistic children is not straightforward therefore, and often involves finding ways of using technologies to promote an educational form of play with an identified developmental purpose. Many technology-based approaches see the intrinsic value of play for children as important in terms of the motivation to engage, but include a high level of adult control over the technology and an emphasis on the instrumental value of play. Technologies are sometimes used for the purpose of developing children's capacity for interaction within simplified virtual environments, to facilitate the functional use of early communicative skills, to encourage social attention and to practice specific social interactions.

Box 3.6   Technology-based approach to play

Somantics/ReacTickles Magic

Somantics and ReacTickles Magic are interactive software applications that facilitate children's playful engagement, using a range of beautifully designed digital interfaces. Children's touch and gesture are responded to and elaborated on digitally, to produce enjoyable and intrinsically motivating sensory experiences of flow and repetition. These tools encourage self-expression and creativity as well as a greater awareness of self and agency. They also allow interactive communication between the user and their parents and teachers (Keay-Bright, 2009).

Play and an inclusive curriculum

It is apparent that many of the approaches to supporting the development of play in children with autism are not easily incorporated into a school-based curriculum. Some are stand-alone programmes that are highly intensive and delivered over the course of many hours in a week, and some are designed to be delivered by a trained and registered specialist or therapist, who is not usually also a class teacher. Some can be delivered only on a one-to-one basis and require a child to be educated outside of the classroom. In terms of inclusive education, there is a danger that the curriculum in relation to the play of autistic children becomes radically different to that which exists for other children and serves to exclude them from ordinary play contexts.

Inclusion concerns the development of educational systems that are able to accommodate all learners, and the challenge of inclusion is the creation of learning opportunities that are suitable for children irrespective of their learning needs or disability. The inclusion agenda arose out of problems associated with 'specialist pedagogies' that have little evidence to support actual effectiveness, undermine children's rights and threaten their educational entitlement to a broad and balanced curriculum. Inclusive practice concerns developing curricula and teaching methods that are accessible to all learners. Within inclusive education, the use of specialized programmes and pedagogies are used only when necessary and not where difference is only perceived to exist or arbitrarily judged as problematic.

Lewis and Norwich (2005) have introduced a framework for thinking about inclusive practice which incorporates three levels of pedagogy:

- *pedagogy that is common to all learners.* This is the dominant pedagogy and must be flexible enough to allow for considerable individual variation;

- *specialist pedagogy* for specific areas of learning and distinct groups of learners. This should replace common pedagogy only when absolutely necessary;
- *individual pedagogy* for learners who have unique needs in some areas.

Lewis and Norwich argue that inclusive practice concerns implementing a common pedagogy that is as far as possible applicable to all. A non-inclusive curriculum is one that excludes children from the outset and uses alternative curricula at the outset to replace what is not available.

A play-based curriculum

Within education, play is seen as of value in relation to children's learning and development, but in ways that reflect the highly integrated and affective nature of play. Engaging in play activity is valuable, not only because children learn through play but also because of its intrinsic qualities. Children are motivated to play, and play promotes emotional health and well-being, and supports social competency and participation. Play is seen as an important way in which children explore the world and create meanings for themselves, but it is not something that can be taught to them by adults. The role of the educational practitioner is to assess and document children's learning through play and plan play-based activities to create further learning opportunities.

A play-based curriculum is one that seeks to provide opportunities to learn through play, but it is child-led and will seek to identify what individually motivates and engages children. An enriched view of play is mostly taken within education, where a wide range of children's play activity – though not all – is seen as educationally relevant, and in which it is recognized that children play in different ways, for different purposes and with their own play preferences. Children are seen as having a right to play and play as having an important role in their interactions, communication and everyday lives. A play-based curriculum is particularly relevant within early years education, but this understanding of the nature and purpose of play operates outside of the early years too.

Disabled children are also seen as having a right to play, and their play preferences are of value and interest to educational practitioners. As with all children, the role of the educational practitioner is to create inclusive contexts for play and learning by assessing the particular interests and capacities of individual children and making provision for these. For children with autism who are engaged in more solitary play, this may be valued in itself as an important leisure pursuit and time spent away from stressful social demands, but planning may also concern providing opportunities to engage in play with others, whether adults or children. Thus, it is possible to see how some of the approaches to play that have been outlined earlier could be used within specialist or individual pedagogies, in the way that Lewis and Norwich envisage it – for example, the use of naturalistic playful engagement and shared communication that is found in relationship-based developmental approaches. Not all approaches to autism and play would fit this educational model, however, and care would need to be taken to ensure that methods did not exclude children with autism from play-based learning.

Much more will be said in Chapter 5 about play-based learning and developing contexts for play within education. Before this, the next chapter will focus on insider accounts of autism and play.

Chapter 4

Autistic perspectives on play and friendship

Focus of this chapter:

- the sensory basis of autistic perception and autism as a culture
- patterns of children's play and interactions as described in autobiographical accounts produced by autistic writers, in relation to pretending, sensory play, social interactions and being friends
- the importance of animals, nature and the sensory-perceptual features of words in autistic children's play cultures
- some issues for practitioners to consider in relation to autistic children's play.

Introduction

The central importance of the internal experience of play makes personal perspectives on play especially significant. Approaches to play tend to focus on outer play behaviours because these are observable, but how play is experienced 'on the inside' is knowledge that is much more reliant on personal accounts. In the literature on autism, a large number of autistic autobiographies exist, but these have been largely overlooked by academic research because of problems associated with using them as reliable data. Autobiography relies largely on memory, which can be unreliable, and often involves a linear narrative that tries to make sense of the writer's life in the present day. It is a retrospective construction that may be influenced by narratives produced by other writers or by present-day concerns and interests. The fact that many autistic autobiographies are co-authored further complicates the issue of whose voice this is.

However, as Billington (2006) points out, the current agenda of partnership working in the helping professions draws attention to the existence of personal narratives and autobiographies, and their importance in guiding practice and giving users a voice within the development of services. Whilst professionals may focus on deficits and ways to address these for the individual, it is the case that many insider accounts provide a counterargument to a 'cure perspective' (Bagatell, 2010), challenging assumptions about what is 'normal' and describing value in difference and diversity. Autistic autobiographies provide information about how the autistic individual perceives and interprets the world, something that the non-autistic professional would otherwise find it hard to know. For this reason, autistic autobiographies are used here to provide insight into experiences of play, playfulness and friendship for a child with autism as a way of helping us think about what play means for the children we support and our role as practitioners.

Autistic perception

Having autism means processing the world in mostly sensory ways that are focused on the look, feel, taste, smell and sound of an object or event, or how the body experiences it in space. Experience of the world tends not to be socially mediated – that is, it is not experienced as social relationships, cultural understandings or recognizable social practices. The sound of the breeze in the trees, for example, may not be experienced as 'summer', 'holiday time' and 'relaxation from school', or the smell of a favourite meal as 'relationship to my mother', 'affection' and 'care'. Experience is often interpreted by an autistic person in terms of the particular configuration of sensory experiences at the moment of perception and so gives rise to highly individualistic ways of making sense of the world. Non-social sensory experience can be rich and very varied, but it tends not to be shareable with other people, who will not have experienced and processed something in the same way.

Tito Mukhopadhyay's description of his perception of a door illustrates this difference well. He describes how on first looking at a door, he does not automatically recognize what it is, that it is a door and therefore a boundary between two rooms and an entry point for people:

> When I enter a new room, which I am entering for the first time, and look at a door, I recognize it as a door, only after a few stages. The first thing I see is its color. If I do not get into a deeper cogitation of its color by defining it as 'yellow', and mentally lining up all the yellow things I know of, including one of my tennis balls when I was seven years old, I move to the shape of the door. And if at all I lay my eyes on the door hinge, I might get distracted by the functions of levers. However, I pull my attention from there and wonder about the function of that yellow, large rectangular object, with levers of the first order, called a hinge. Why is that yellow, large rectangular object with levers there? I mentally answer the question, 'It has allowed me to come inside that room, and can be opened or closed. And what else can that be, other than a door'.
>
> (2008: 95)

Autistic perception involves experiencing everything within a scene at once, not distilling what is being perceived according to ideas and concepts brought to the act of perception. It is a form of 'gestalt perception' where a scene is processed as a whole, with any change to this experienced as a complete change to the fundamental meaning of the scene (Bogdashina, 2003). Gunilla Gerland, in her vivid account of growing up as a child with autism, describes the overwhelming nature of her sensory experience, one that impacted on her globally and got in the way of her learning. 'I heard everything', she writes, 'as if it were one complete sound', the teacher talking, the rustle of paper, the scraping of chairs and cars outside the classroom. She describes having to create a mental 'wall' to compartmentalise her thinking and focus on just one thing:

> Every sudden sound meant risking losing hold of the wall. With one 'hand' I held up the wall between sounds, and with the other I tried to clean out my ear so that no new rubbishy sounds got in the way of what I was trying to listen to. With my third 'hand', the one I almost didn't have, I tried at the same time to sort out the information, the content of what I was listening to.
>
> (1997: 94)

The differences autistic people experience in terms of perception and sensory processing are numerous. Common amongst them are hypersensitivity to sensory stimuli – for example, loud noises and certain textures – or conversely *hypo*sensitivity, which describes a low state of sensory arousal and a seeking out of stimulation. There may fluctuation between these two states as well as fragmented perception, where only parts of objects are processed – for example, only some parts of a conversation are heard or some parts of a face seen. Autistic people may experience delayed or distorted perception where, for example, people are seen with huge hands and mouths. It is also the case that autism is more closely associated with agnosia, which is the inability to recognize ordinary objects, and with synaesthesia, where perception occurs across two or more sensory modalities – for example, numbers perceived as colours. The problems associated with sensory processing, such as intense sensory overload for the individual, may result in a state of 'sensory shutdown' and perhaps even complete withdrawal. For many autistic writers, however, the experience of their sensory world is not always one of disorder and difficulty, but often one of fascination and pleasure.

The differential nature of autistic perception interferes with cultural learning and with the sharing of 'common sense' meanings of the world (Trevarthen and Daniel, 2006). Autistic accounts describe the ways in which it is the perception of the *social* meanings that is problematic. The flat surface of a table is not necessarily a 'teacher's desk' or somewhere to eat, the use of the corridor of a school is not determined by time, and a line on the floor is not somewhere to wait for the next instruction. People can be experienced as objects too, not as subjects with internal states and thoughts of their own that can be communicated and understood. This is powerfully conveyed in relation to human faces that are often described as experienced by an autistic person with no sense of meaning. Gerland (1997) writes of her experience of being left alone with another child whom she did not know. 'She was just an empty face, a younger sister, a little kid looking at me in a silly way that I couldn't interpret' (page 81), a disturbing enough experience for Gerland that resulted in her hitting out at the girl. Faces are typically described as hard or impossible to distinguish one from another, or as anything other than shapes, colours and shadows. It is sometimes said that it is impossible to see a 'person' in the face (Blackman, 2009). The experience of human faces can be a frightening one, of activity, movement, faces looming or thrusting themselves, and a jolt out of a more pleasurable sensory experience of another person:

> I ran my hand down her plait. She looked around at me and I was frightened by the way that her face was joined to her hair. I wanted to touch her hair, not her.
> (Williams, 1992: 20)

Autism as a culture

In trying to understand autistic perception it is possible to see why predictability, familiarity and orderliness of experience are so basic as needs for an autistic person. For many autistic writers, the ongoing difficulty of orienting oneself to the social world, with its many hidden social meanings and ever-changing social practices, in addition to sensory processing and body orientation issues, results in an experience of a world that is not stable. Typically, the ability to cope with an unstable world is described as requiring the experience of sameness, and not of novelty or change. If the experience of the table or of the corridor or of the person is always the same, then there is the possibility of gaining an understanding of social meaning, much as Mukhopadhyay learned the meaning of the yellow door. If orderliness of experience is not available, the impact on the individual is often described in momentous terms: as a state of panic or terror, and as a devastating loss of a sense of self.

Though autism is highly individual, with great variation existing in the ways in which the sensory and social world is experienced, this distinctive desire for sameness and predictability has given rise to the idea of autism as a culture. Culture refers to shared ways of understanding, communicating and behaving. Straus (2013), amongst others, argues that autistic perception results in a culture of everyday life which is shared across the autistic population. He outlines the following as distinctive features of autism as a culture:

- *local coherence*, where an autistic person experiences an event as 'full and complete' in itself and does not interpret it in the light of social concepts and categories that exist outside of that event;

- a *preference for repetition*, where events are preferably experienced in exactly the same way each time and where change is avoided;
- *private meanings* that are created by an autistic person and that are idiosyncratic and unusual, but experienced by someone as pleasurable and sufficient.

Viewing autism as a culture provides a different perspective on behaviour and puts forward the idea that what we see in the behaviour of autistic people flows naturally from their subjective experience of the world. For example, according to this view, 'rhythmic stereotypies', such as hand flapping, rocking back and forth, and ritualistic touching or arranging of objects, could be seen as a form of cultural practice that autistic people employ partly to manage their presence in a complex and overwhelming social world and to maintain a sense of self in the face of the instability of their experience (Nazeer, 2007).

Play cultures of autistic children

We are engaged here in thinking about play, a behaviour which is influenced by the individual's experience of the world and by their sense of self. It stands to reason that a differential experience of the world and of self, as described by autistic writers, will have an impact on the experience of play. Play is often described in pejorative terms in narrative accounts written by autistic people, as something imposed upon them, adult-directed and repetitiously boring (Kedar, 2012). However, many autistic autobiographies provide descriptions of voluntary, pleasurable and absorbing activities that the writer carried out when they were young. These are described in terms of a connection to the world – whether sensory or social – and a rich experience of self, and so would appear to fulfil the criteria of play.

Patterns of such experience, identified across autobiographies, would suggest specific play cultures that exist in similar ways for different individuals. Indeed, in reading autistic autobiographies it appears to be the case that a distinctive play style does exist, one that is sensory-based rather than socially mediated and concerns exploration of the world as it is autistically perceived and experienced. It is these patterns of play experience that are explored more fully ahead, using personal narratives produced by autistic writers.

Autistic play: Pretending

In autobiographies produced by autistic writers, there are many descriptions of how the writer as a child participated in play situations that involved imagination and pretence, though the way in which this happened is characterised by difference. Jeannie Davide-Rivera describes a form of pretend play that she favoured which involved real objects, hyperreal representations and a playing out of actual routines. She was unable to play with dolls except for Baby Joey, an anatomically correct and 'controversial toy' to those around her because it looked exactly like a real baby. Playing schools involved setting out the 'pretend school' as a space that was very close to real life:

> I spent hours setting the tables and chairs just right, arranging them so my students could see the chalk board. I collected textbooks, papers, pencils, crayons, chalk, and erasers. I gathered black and white notebooks for the class to practice writing their multiplication tables. Pretend things would not do; I needed real supplies . . . By the time my classroom was finished and ready to *play* my friends had run off.
>
> (2012: 42)

Daniel Tammet (2006) describes how he enjoyed playing ironing with his siblings, a game which involved him using a real iron that had been switched off and allowed to cool. Tammet recalls that his siblings were keen to join in with him as he ironed real clothes, one sibling using a spray, another folding the clothes and a third piling them into categories of t-shirts, jumpers and trousers. Tammet remarks that he and his siblings loved his ironing game, playing it repeatedly and often for hours at a time.

An aspect of this autistic pretending appears to concern a preoccupation with the orderliness of objects and of everyday routines. Davide-Rivera (2012) writes of wanting a life-sized Barbie head with long blonde hair, 'not to play with', but so that she could arrange the brushes and make-up that came with the doll. Davide-Rivera describes how her only interest in creating pretend scenarios was to recreate her life, but in a more orderly, predictable and, as she writes, 'better' way. Other writers refer to the same purpose of play when they describe arranging and labelling objects in pretend play to reflect their real-life preference of systems and order (Gerland, 1997).

There is a sense from these descriptions that what is being imagined and explored is reality as it exists if one has autism. It is a reality that is highly visual in nature and gives rise to make-believe acts that are notable for their visual quality, where what is created is most appreciable for the shape and overall look. For Davide-Rivera, her stacking of blocks was an attempt to recreate the New York skyscrapers she saw from her father's car as they drove across the Brooklyn Bridge. Mukhopadhyay (2008) describes his joy at recreating in play the staircases he loved to climb in real life, using blocks for the steps and cabbages to climb up and fall down them, 'again and again'. He played this game with his mother repeatedly and remarks of it, 'I loved eating cabbages'.

Mukhopadhyay's extraordinary account of his mental game of planting nails in a wall also raises the possibility that the act of imagining for an autistic person is closely tied up with a heightened capacity for remembering visual and other sensory detail. Mukhopadhyay found his game highly enjoyable, mentally absorbing and strongly visual, and reliant on an ability to keep track of what was being imagined:

> I sat a whole day in a classroom, planting mental nails all over the walls of that room. While I planted those mental nails, I kept a count of them. I knew that those nails never existed in real dimensions, but when I planted them I experienced their hardness and their blackened shine. They kept my mind busy the whole day . . . I mentally placed them very close to each other, as if they were a plate full of mustard seeds. People walked in and out of the classroom many times. Perhaps I did, too. But I was not bothered. I was very busy, as my mind carefully fixed those nails close to each other, counting and concentrating on the task . . . Planting mental nails and remembering the numbers and allotting a place to each nail needed a whole lot of staring at the wall.
>
> (2008: 122–4)

Autistic play: Sensory engagement

Strongly sensory processes of play are described in accounts of autistic pretending, but also in descriptions of other types of playful activity. Many writers refer to the pleasure they derived when young from arranging things, tidying up, stacking coins to make 'shining, trembling towers' (Tammet, 2006), carefully ordering card collections, and arranging letters and numbers. 'I loved those alphabet cards', writes Gerland (1997: 47). 'They were so clean and clear, on white cardboard with red edges'. Autistic writers often provide accounts of pleasurable leisure activities that gave them a sense of well-being as a child, and many of these involved an intense form of sensory engagement. Williams (1992) notes her love as a child of heavy oak doors, polished floors, coloured glass 'high up', trees that hung over the playground, and the hair of her friend Elizabeth. She also lists amongst her playful pursuits listening to gravel, looking through coloured plastic, staring through the cat, getting lost in wallpaper, following lines and fences and feeling statues (Williams, 2008). In a similar vein, Lawson (2000) describes how, as a girl, she enjoyed watching the light gleam from the silver mudguards of her bike as she spun the wheels round and round. Other favourite activities were thinking about bright colours and different shades of light, rubbing wax crayons over paper and making scratched patterns, and playing with a spinning top by 'listening to its whirly sound'.

Lawson claims that it is from these sensory-based activities that feelings of safety, comfort and a connection to 'life and feeling' were derived. This is a theme found in many writers' works, where sensory engagement is identified as fundamental to a sense of self and the experience that makes the individual feel truly alive. Sensory engagement is described as underpinning a sense of calmness and stability in the individual and so ensuring good mental health and well-being. Gerland writes of her intense enjoyment of curved objects:

> My love for curved things began early, long before it became so vital to hold them. I liked bends – they were so soft and, well, curved. I felt a need for them and they gave me some kind of satisfaction. A curved thing had something calming about it, a wholly obvious feeling . . . I kept touching things all the time – poking my fingers into or under bottles, sofa arms and door-handles, rubbing my palms against turned banisters. I simply had to touch all these things that had the curve I needed . . . All I knew was that what I did, I did out of necessity, vital necessity.
>
> (1997: 11–12)

Ido Kedar (2012) describes how he is forced to stop and look at water in the sunlight or at lights blinking because 'it's so artistically awesome'. He describes how he can see 'woven patterns of shapes and colours' in the lights and other details that are 'lovely' and 'amazing'. His synesthetic experience of music, where he experiences musical notes as shapes, lights and colours as well as sound, is particularly pleasing to him. He describes listening to music as a 'full sensory experience of sound, sight and temperature' that causes him to feel hot and cold, to experience total absorption and to see 'a show in 3-D'. In evocative descriptions of sensory absorption, Mukhopadhyay too describes the many ways in which he experiences sensory highs. His fascination with ceiling fans, for example, provides an intoxicating mixture of visual and kinaesthetic pleasure and a powerful sense of bodily self:

> I would watch the opaque blades move faster and faster, as the fan would pick up acceleration, and then become transparent in the color of air, so that the ceiling could be seen clearly. Then it would look like a transparent circle, moving below the ceiling . . . I would stand right below it, and rotate my body as fast as I could, wondering whether I too became as transparent as the fan. It felt wonderful to think that way. I could gather my body parts while I rotated, so that I could feel my arms, legs, and fingers, in total control.
>
> (2008: 59–60)

Mukhopadhyay, Kedar and other autistic writers express some caution about 'getting lost' in sensory engagement. They describe self-stimulatory or 'stimming' experiences of prolonged or complete absorption that mean 'I am lost in a sensory world of big soaring feelings' (Kedar, 2012: 42). It is absorption that perhaps differs in intensity from the absorption described in definitions of play. This also refers to immersion in an enjoyable and energizing focus activity that involves a mental state of 'getting lost'. However, there is not the same sense of being unable to disengage that some writers with autism describe as their experience and the reason why they must exercise some control over getting 'too lost' (Kedar, 2012).

Reflective task

Find objects of different shapes and with interesting textures – for example, a round plate with a reflective surface, a chopstick with a tassel on the end, a patterned fan. Include objects that you can look through, spin and wave.

Within a group, pass round one object at a time. Ask group members to 'transform' the object by acting out a pretence that it is something else, the pretence suggested by the shape or other property of the object. For example, a plate may be used as a steering wheel, a hat or Frisbee, a chopstick as a magic wand, umbrella or comb for the hair. Group members can be encouraged to say what the object is as an action is performed.

Pass each object again, this time asking group members to play with the object in a sensory way. Note what happens to the language content in this second round – that is, that sensory play does not involve language (though there may be vocalizations) and group members have nothing they can identify and name.

Attachment to objects, animals and nature

The intense sensory experience of objects in autism is often described in more powerful terms than social, interpersonal connections. Autistic autobiographies testify to experiences of the anthropomorphism of objects that are as alive and animated as people. 'Moments are defined by what your senses are compelled to attend to', writes Mukhopadhyay, ' . . . a pen peeping out from the pile of papers, perhaps wishing to have a voice so that it could say aloud, "Here I am! Here I am!" ' (2008: 53). By virtue of the erect and moving 'character' of cranes, Gerland said she was convinced they were alive. 'I could see from my window that they had moved their heads during the night. I thought that people used them in the daytime and then they were able to live freely at night' (1997: 36).

The intensity of sensory engagement in autism appears to give rise to relationships to non-human things that are as enduring and deeply felt as attachment relationships are for non-autistic people (Davidson and Smith, 2009). This is particularly the case for relationships to animals, which are often described as intimate, empathetic and emotionally satisfying. Lawson writes that 'Although I was unable to relate to other children . . . with animals it was different'. As a young girl, her relationship to her cat, Sandy, was loving and a 'definite connection', whilst she was 'inseparable' from her red-haired dog, Rusty.

Temple Grandin, an autistic writer and expert on animal behaviour, writes that she feels closer to animals than to people. She claims that her autism enables her to 'think the way animals think' and achieve an empathetic understanding that supports a deep connection, deeper than anything she experiences with human beings (Grandin and Johnson, 2005). Grandin's particular attachment to cattle is based for her on a shared sense of the world, one that is sensorily oriented and straightforward in terms of emotion. As Davidson and Smith (2009) note, this attachment relationship is for Grandin a communicative one where she feels able to make sense of cow experience and 'translate' it for non-autistic people. They point out that Grandin's success as an animal behaviourist, underlined by the fact that her designs constitute half of all cattle handling facilities in the US, powerfully supports these claims.

In autistic autobiographies, nature is also described in terms of intimate and joyful connection that could be viewed as an attachment relationship. Kedar (2012) notes that his experience of nature is antithetical to and a welcome relief from social relationships. He finds social noise – people's talk, movement and the sounds of the city – an overwhelming 'din' that makes him feel 'haywire inside', but the sound of the wind in the trees, ocean waves and birdsong provides a welcome reprieve from this. Williams (1992) writes of her harmonious and pleasurable exploration of nature around her home. As a young girl she would spend the day 'exploring' by herself, watching the fish in a neighbour's pond, dancing in the garden, eating pot-plants, and throwing rose petals 'high in the air' to 'walk through them as though they were stars' (page 13). Lawson explains that nature is a constant, calm and reassuring presence, without the interruptions and noise that are present in social space. A particular love for the sea is supported by the predictability of experience that exists in standing on the seashore:

> I just loved the sea. It made me feel safe; it was comforting and was always there . . . As I approached the sandy shore I noticed how calmly

the water washed over the grains of sand and pulled them back into the sea as it retreated. The movement of constant washing, pushing forward and retrieval fascinated me and I could watch it for hours . . . I felt life was different beside the sea: there were no demanding voices, no instructions to follow, no commands to obey, no competition or fights with my sisters over chairs.

(2000: 23–4)

For educational practitioners working with autistic children, it is hard to underestimate the importance of natural environments. Mukhopadhyay writes of his belief that nature *is* autism because of some strongly shared characteristics:

I made a whole list of things that I thought had autism. The curtains that moved in the wind, the big and small leaves that moved a little more with the air because of their suspended positions, the little bits of paper, or the pages of an open book under a fan were classified as autistic. They were affected with autism because they flapped, because they would not respond to any blocks, because they did not talk.

(2008: 27–8)

Autistic socializing and friendship

Just as there is an anthropomorphic sense of objects in autism, so people can be experienced not as subjects with minds and thoughts of their own but as objects. The overwhelming sense of another person might involve an awareness of their physical or sensory self: the tone of their voice, the 'shape of their smile' or the length of their hair (Lawson, 2000: 40). Williams (1992) writes of her strong attachment to the sensory experience of another person as well as to the objects they owned. She writes, 'For me, the people I liked *were* their things', and describes the love she felt for her grandmother as based on her camphor smell, the chains she wore round her neck, her 'husky laughing voice' and the knitted things she wore that Williams 'could put my fingers through' (page 5).

In autistic autobiographies, getting to know a person is often described as a process of getting to know their outsides. Gerland (1997) writes that the hypersensitivity she felt in her teeth meant she would ask people if she could bite their arms and remarks that, 'strangely enough', some people allowed this. Closeness to another person is described not as a state of interest in and concern for what they are thinking or feeling but as more of a sense of alignment within sensory engagement. Davide-Rivera (2012) writes of her 'all or nothing' friend Vanessa, with whom she felt an unspoken but perfect attunement and a shared 'logic of behaviour'. Vanessa went along with Davide-Rivera's transgressive activities, though no discussion about this is described and no detailed description of Vanessa 'as a person' is provided within the text. Davide-Rivera writes of the intense pleasure she derived from the friendship and the play they carried out together, which also involved acting, singing and performing intricately coordinated dance moves. However, she also writes of her deeply felt regret that she was unable to participate in more socially based interpersonal interaction when Vanessa's father died, not being able to think of what to say or do to comfort her friend.

There is a growing interest in the particular form human interaction takes for autistic people. The experience of another person outlined by Davide-Rivera evokes the idea of 'interactive stimming' as introduced by the autistic writer and campaigner Jim Sinclair (2005). Interactive stimming refers to a particular form of spontaneous interaction for people with autism, in which interaction with other people is experienced as synchronized, rhythmic and pleasurable, but not as interpersonally felt. Williams provides a good example of this when she writes of her enjoyment of play with her friend Sandra:

> She'd laugh, I'd laugh, we'd laugh. We'd sit side by side and scream in each other's ear. It made me laugh because it tickled, and I really didn't care what it was that she was screaming; she was the first person to play my games. Through playtime and lunchtime Sandra and I would drink as much water as we could, until we felt we would bust. We'd choke ourselves until we turned blue, coughing and struggling to breathe. We would try to push our eyes in, in order to see colours, and we would scream and scream until our throats were red raw.
>
> (1992: 21)

Sinclair (2005) has also introduced the idea of 'autistic socializing' to describe the fact that a natural form of interaction for people with autism exists which has characteristic features. Autistic socializing involves a preference for non-face-to-face interactions, reduced amounts of back-and-forth conversation and a greater tolerance of one person engaging in talk about their special interests (Ochs and Solomon, 2010). There may also be greater mediation of friendship by non-human contact – for example, through computers or animals – and a greater attraction to people who are experienced as quiet and gentle. There may be a preference for experiencing interaction on a one-to-one basis rather than in groups. Indeed, for some autistic writers, playing within groups of children is often described as overwhelming, where other children are experienced as 'an indistinguishable confusion of arms and legs' that 'frightened me and wore me out' (Gerland, 1997: 41). Many writers testify to their need to experience closeness to a friend and their enjoyment of shared playful activity, but only if it occurs on a one-to-one basis:

> Friends are time-consuming, dramatic, and exhausting. They take energy, and work. I have never been able to maintain casual relationships, acquaintances, or contacts . . . My choice of friend is total; all or nothing. I am an all-the-way, all-the-time friend, or nothing at all. My friend will be totally immersed in my life, or completely cut-off.
>
> (Davide-Rivera, 2012: 61)

Patterns of friendships exist within the literature produced by autistic writers. Friends are often described as similarly rejected children or as fellow outsiders to social groups, who are 'on the same wavelength' and appreciate interests that differ from those of other children. Williams (1992) describes her friend Terry, who shared her interest of cats, collecting 'bits and pieces from garbage' and riding on buses. She also describes another friend, Trish, who was quiet, shy and gentle, and happy to watch as Williams engaged in her favourite activities of dancing and twirling. A common trait of being happy to go along with things and follow Williams in her favoured pursuits describes both these friendships, but this is not something that Williams experienced in relationships with other children, so much so that, in high school, she was forced to go round and plead with people to be her friend.

Along with Williams, Davide-Rivera (2012) attests to the importance of characters in books and other imaginary friends, who felt more real to her and enjoyable as companions than any real-life counterpart. She writes of the vivid presence in her house of the baseball players she loved to watch on television and how she engaged in ball play more successfully with them than with her father. Of the ten imaginary puppies she also had as friends, she describes her overwhelming panic when she 'saw' them scurry out of the family car as it was stopped by the side of the road. She let out a 'blood-curdling scream' when only some of the puppies returned, but was consoled when her father and her imaginary baseball friends eventually found the missing three dogs.

Enjoyable processes of play with friends and siblings often depend on the non-autistic play partner's attunement to 'autistic thinking' and capacity to invent suitable if unusual games. Gerland's sister, Kerstin, is described as particularly creative in this respect, her invention of fantasy jungles in their bedroom proving an exciting and much-loved game for Gerland:

> With bedclothes, chairs and her imagination, [Kerstin] built and told the story. 'This is a jungle and that's a tiger and you're a little girl who's got lost' . . . Sometimes, following her instructions, I might help build, but usually I was

the one to fetch the building materials from various rooms in the house. I was quite satisfied with this division of roles and regarded our games as mutual exchanges. But when the building was finished, the game was over. I was not the sort of playmate who could go on spinning the yarn and playing in the jungle once it was finished.

(1997: 39)

Good play partners are described as tolerant of playing games repetitively and happy to engage in play with a significant sensorimotor element. Gerland describes the game of 'cars', which involved her and her sister lying along the sofa with their feet pressed together and making driving noises, and another game that involved Gerland suspended on her sister's knees 'with just the amount of physical contact that I could cope with' (page 38).

Gerland's account of playing with her sister gives a fascinating insight into how play can be experienced in a differential way by the non-autistic play partner. Gerland writes of her sister Kerstin that 'she found a way of playing with me that gave *her* something'. She describes a game called Sausage Cat and Esmerelda, in which her sister and a friend dressed up as these two characters and pretended they were Gerland's guardian angels. Gerland explains that her autism meant that she 'swallowed it hook, line and sinker', truly believing they were angels because they said so and because they wore different sets of clothes (page 121). As she grew older, Gerland realized the deceit but wanted to carry on playing the game. Kerstin and her friend continued to play but only half-heartedly since they no longer experienced the excitement of playing with Gerland's real belief and fear. Gerland's account is reminiscent of accounts of playfighting provided by non-autistic siblings in which the experience of play is a peculiarly exciting one, of heightened energy and a frightening sense of real danger. It also highlights that fact that it is possible for other children to 'tune in' to autism in negative ways, achieving a good understanding of how their peer with autism makes sense of the world, what makes them frightened or react in certain ways, and using this knowledge to tease, upset and bully.

Autistic play: Physical play

Gerland's description of the game of cars that she played with her sister serves to remind us that motor play is an especially important play activity for children with autism. Research finds that children with autism engage in more spontaneous sensorimotor play than other children, showing a preference for sensory, physical, and rough-and-tumble play (Holmes and Willoughby,

2005). Autistic autobiographies bear this out, describing the ways in which sensory-perceptual-motor play provides an easy way of being with someone that does not involve a high level of verbal content or complex social interaction. Williams (1992) describes her younger brother, Tom, as having similar play interests to her own, which included spinning round and round, falling to the ground and jumping on the beds in their house. 'Sometimes we would lie down head-first', she writes, 'and come thumping down the stairs, our heads hitting every step, upside down, until we crashed to the bottom' (pp. 24–5). Davide-Rivera (2012) similarly describes enjoyable play with three neighbourhood friends with whom she performed dance moves in their backyard. Her friends created a stage, dressed in tutus and 'twirled around like the ballerinas we were', in endless enjoyment of the game. Davide-Rivera and her friends put on shows for their parents, but she writes, 'I wonder if they ever tired of our shows. We seem to be always be putting on a show, and many times to an empty audience' (page 31).

Within many accounts, the experience of physical play is described as providing an enjoyable and exciting sense of bodily self. The twirling and tiptoeing of ballet play, the vigorousness of climbing, and sensory disruption of hanging upside down or spinning round and round are all experiences of play that are described as giving pleasurable bodily feedback. Both Kedar (2012) and Gerland (1997) describe swimming as a preferred activity that gives them gentle feedback of their body in water and an experience of their limbs not felt outside of the water. Both these writers record some individual difficulty in relation to physical play, however. For Kedar, he finds that his weak postural control, body sense and coordination make some activities difficult, such as throwing a ball in basketball, but that walking, working out, jumping and riding a bike are accessible and pleasurable. For Gerland, her experience of physical play was difficult when other children were present. Though she enjoyed climbing a particular climbing frame – one shaped like an igloo with a hole at the top – she found that the presence of other children on the frame interfered with her concentration and made the act of climbing an impossible one. She writes, 'Carrying out anything to do with movement required my total presence of mind, my total control' (Gerland, 1997: 76).

Lawson's enjoyment of continuous running in the playground at school appears to have served a similar sensory-perceptual-motor experience:

> Faster, faster . . . my heart was pounding as my shoe-shod feet ran around the vast playground. The bitumen floor of the school playground intrigued me and I noticed that as I ran it seemed to run with me. At play times, I ran and ran and ran, giggling out loud as I did so.
>
> (2000: 29)

Writing about the 'sensory geographies' of autism, Davidson and Henderson (2010) note that for autistic people their physical use of space is partly about regaining a sense of self in the face of social disorientation. They describe rhythmic rocking, tiptoe walking and hand flapping as important ways of managing the 'painful effects of involvement in social space'. It is questionable therefore whether some aspects of physical activity for children with autism could be described as 'play', and may more accurately be described as 'survival', though some play theories put the value of play as high as this.

Autistic play: Playing with words

Though language and communication are characteristic areas of difficulty for people with autism, autistic autobiographies clearly illustrate the fact that playing with the sensory qualities of words is a feature of autistic pleasure and play. Davide-Rivera (2012) describes her love of creating 'perfectly constructed' handwriting, when she did not think of what the words meant, but only that each letter looked good. Williams (1992) also describes her love of letters and the visual way they fit together to make words. Other writers describe their enjoyment of the sounds made by words. Gerland writes that the rhythm of poetry 'appealed to my sense of order and my desire for predictability', and that inserting full stops, colons and commas in her writing was like using musical instruments. Though she was not always aware of the 'social dimensions' of what she read, she loved words nevertheless for their length, shape and sound quality, collecting new ones and storing them in her memory. Several writers describe their enjoyment of being engaged with others in the playing of word games – for example, Williams playing Scrabble with her mother and Kedar playing the word-guessing game Taboo at a Thanksgiving dinner, when 'people could see I am very clever'.

Dawn Prince-Hughes describes her complete fascination for words when she was young, enjoying the sounds particularly of difficult words. A favourite game involved her relatives shouting out a long word and then Prince-Hughes calling out this word repeatedly as she made a circuit of her grandparents' house on her tricycle. She did this to invest each word with a personal meaning, associating it to sensory and much-loved features of the house:

> The word would seem different somehow, taking on new properties, as I passed my cherished landmarks. 'Hippopotamus!' I would say as I passed . . . my grandparents' bedroom, where the word would absorb the comfort of my grandparents' bed, their clothing, the beauty of my grandmother's vanity table, and the smell of cedar drawers; then on to the bathroom yelling

'Hippopotamus!' where the word would absorb the smell of antiseptic, toilet bowl cleaner, baby powder, perfume and toothpaste.

(2004: 18)

It is not surprising to learn that writing for many autistic writers has a special meaning, beyond the visual quality and sound of the words. Writing is described by some as a form of communication that is easier and more natural than verbal communication, a form of expression that is less fast-paced than talking and more manageable in its non-face-to-face social orientation. Many autistic auto-biographies describe enjoyable leisure time spent in the library, reading books and writing stories. Mukhopadhyay (2008), for example, who has achieved considerable fame for his narrative writings but also for his poetry, movingly describes his 'slow by slow' experience of writing that allows him to gather together the 'pieces and bits' of daily life and process them within his own time-scale, and so very gradually make sense of his world.

Implications for practice

The different ways in which the sensory and social world is experienced by autistic people mean that a single 'autistic style' will not describe the whole population, but patterns of experience do exist. This appears to be the case for the play and friendships of children with autism. Children with autism do play and do have friendships, but often with a slightly different purpose or conducted in a distinctive style. We should be careful about seeing children with autism as a completely separate group, however. In autism theory and practice, there has been a tendency to describe autistic experience in absolute terms rather than as on a continuum of difference. Taking the issue of imaginary friends as an example, it is the case that some autistic writers mention the fact that they had an imaginary friend as a child. But this should not lead to the conclusion that *all* autistic children have imaginary friends, since many autistic writers do not describe this experience. Nor should it be read as something that is 'peculiarly autistic'. The existence of imaginary friends for children without autism is actually quite high, with some studies estimating that as many as 41 per cent of all children have some sort of imaginary companion during their childhood (Taylor, 1999).

Table 4.1 suggests *possible* issues to consider in relation to children's engagement in play. Like all children, children with autism are different from each other and do not constitute a homogeneous group. These are issues, therefore, that might relate to the way in which an autistic child engages with different forms of play in your setting, and it might be helpful to consider some of these points when reflecting on practice and provision.

Table 4.1 Points to consider in relation to autistic children's play cultures

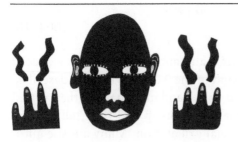

Sensory play
This is the most natural form of play for a child with autism and will probably be richly experienced. Objects may be experienced as 'alive' and more attractive to play with than people because they are less confusing or threatening. There is the possibility that sensory play is the primary experience in what appears to be another type of play – for example, doll play that does not concern pretence but an engagement with the sensory qualities of the doll. The emotional experience of play may be intense, pleasurable and relaxing, and provide an important expression of a sensory self. However, the possibility of the child getting lost in their sensory play is something to bear in mind.

Physical play
Another preferred form of play that is able to provide an enjoyable bodily sense of self. It can also involve a manageable social experience of another person, with reduced verbal content and clearer social interaction in the play. Difficulty may be experienced in terms of coordinating parts of the body to perform certain physical activities, especially when other people are present.

Rough and tumble
A form of play that gives strong muscular feedback, especially for children who are hyposensitive. The play is dependent on a good 'fit' with the play partner, whether adult or child, who has an understanding of what constitutes enjoyable bodily experience for the individual child and who can accept fewer social cues within the play. This form of play may be experienced by non-autistic children as particularly exciting and 'on the edge', though it may more often slip into real fighting and conflict.

Construction play
A preferred form of play involving manipulating objects to create new structures. These may be mostly appreciable in terms of their look, shape or sensory function – for example, to look through, feel the edges of or enjoy as a visual pattern. Construction may be inventive and novel, and an important feature of pretend play – for example, pretence involving a highly detailed model of an object that is significant within the narrative, or involving the construction of the pretend play space.

Rule-based play
There may be difficulties in relation to the rules that exist within a game, especially if they are unspoken or not clearly visible, though once understood play may be enjoyably experienced. Difficulty may also exist around the enforcement of rules, the child insisting on the 'correct way to play' and not allowing a game to be played flexibly.

Risk taking
The concept of risk may be differentially understood by the child with autism and their behaviour experienced by others as socially inappropriate or unacceptable. For example, the child with autism may not have the same understanding as typically developing children of the need to perform risky play away from the surveillance of adults as a way of avoiding sanction and control.

Competitive play
There may be problems around winning and losing, some children interpreting 'to lose' as meaning the same as 'to be wrong' or 'to be bad'. For some children, competitive play may never be experienced as an enjoyable form of play and they may benefit from 'competing against themselves' or from the introduction of non-competitive games.

(Continued)

Table 4.1 (Continued)

Language play
Play may be more concerned with the sounds and rhythms of words rather than any social meanings. Jokes and jeers may be a feature, but ones that poke fun at the 'nonsensical' nature of words, phrases, social norms, understandings and ways of doing things in the non-autistic world.

Play using the arts
This may be favoured by some children with autism – for example, drawing, dancing and role play – and may provide a clear structure and purpose for play interactions.

Pretend play
The nature of what is imagined may reflect an autistic sensory-perceptual perspective on the world, one that is less concerned with people, their roles and relationships, and more with the arrangement of objects. Pretence may concern playing out experiences of sameness and orderliness in terms of routine. Shared intentions in play may be dependent on the level of competency in social communication unless one player takes the lead and clearly directs what is happening in the play.

Chapter 5

Developing inclusive contexts for play and friendship

Focus of this chapter:

- play as a valuable context for social learning and development, and as a space for leisure and positive self-experience
- the role of the teacher as supporter, mediator and active play partner in relation to autistic children's play
- methods in assessment for learning in relation to play and for investigating children's play cultures in your setting
- developing inclusive play contexts and supporting play-based learning for children with autism
- effective ways of supporting children's friendships.

Inclusive education and children's play

Play is seen as a critical context for learning in education, where children are highly motivated to invest themselves and their ideas, explore, make sense of experience, use their skills and learn. Play is seen as integral to all aspects of children's development, including intellectual, social and physical growth, language and communication, and emotional health and well-being. Play supports social sharing and children's experiences of relatedness to other people, which in turn gives them an awareness of other points of view and allows them to take a thinking stance upon the world. Children engage with other children through play, using play for the purpose of communication and shared meaning, and as a way of enjoying each other's company and engaging even more. Play experience is associated with feelings of safety and security and is always accompanied by positive emotional states, pleasurable experiences of relationship, absorption and creativity. Thus play also supports personal growth and is used by children as a form of self-expression, emotion regulation and response to stress. Educational approaches to play view it as having instrumental value, in that it has developmental purpose, but also intrinsic value for children, as a source of leisure, entertainment, relaxation and enjoyment.

The role of the teacher is to create opportunities for children to learn through play. They do this by observing children and reflecting on their play experience, taking into consideration such things as the ideas children are using in their play, what interests them and what individual meanings children are creating through play. Teachers and other educational practitioners are careful in their approach to children's play since the mere presence of an adult can bring a situation of play to an end. Instead, they observe from the sidelines, questioning children about their play outside of the play situation, or adopting a less powerful role of 'play partner' and following the child's lead. Research into effective pedagogy in the early years where a play-based curriculum operates finds that good teachers carry out 'behind the scenes' work, organizing and resourcing play-based learning and facilitating cooperative play routines (Siraj-Blatchford et al., 2002). In this way, teachers are at their most effective as educational practitioners and have the most impact on children's learning and development.

In reflecting on children's play experience, teachers will be concerned with what children are doing in their play, rather than identifying what they are not doing or 'deficit areas of play'. Teaching and learning are a process of seeing what children know and can do and building on these capacities. Autistic perspectives on play, some of which have been described in Chapter 4, remind us of the importance of recognizing the diversity that exists in play experience for children and of not making assumptions about what play means for the individual child. All children's play activity is of interest to teachers and has educational value since it provides insight into their experience and provides substance for further learning.

An inclusive educational approach to the play of autistic children follows the same practice used with all children. The play of a child with autism will be seen as having intrinsic value to the child – for example, as an expression of self, form of self-regulation and experience of well-being. For this purpose, recognition will need to be given to the play preferences of the individual child and the particular ways in which children create meaning in play. Educational practitioners may need to work harder to understand what these are in the case of a child with autism and acknowledge that some meanings are sensory-based more than socially derived. They may also need to introduce more in the way of sensory-based play materials and develop the play space in particular ways. However, all children with autism are at least partly socially engaged and sensitive support for children's play can lead to enjoyable experiences of social inclusion and important social learning and development.

Teacher as supporter, mediator and play partner

From their research into inclusive play, Theodorou and Nind (2010) identify three roles the teacher carries out to support children with autism and their peers in play:

- *teacher as supporter* – the teacher gets involved in children's play to ensure that play continues and that the child with autism is included. The teacher as supporter may suggest an action or role for a child to perform that is relevant to the play activity, model behaviour as a way of supporting children's cooperation with each other, or comment in a positive manner on an event within the play as a way of elucidating what is happening between players. These interventions will happen only occasionally and in a gentle manner to ensure that the teacher does not dominate the play and children's participation within it, and so be perceived by children to be evaluating their play.

- *teacher as mediator* – the teacher acts when misunderstandings arise between players and there is an indication of potential conflict. This is as a way of supporting children to be able to continue playing together and to ensure that one child is not excluded from the play. Again, the actions of the teacher are minimal and positively framed to reduce any sense of adult dominance.

- *teacher as active play partner* – the teacher engages in the play scenario, acting as an active but equal playmate. The teacher in the role of play partner follows what children are doing in their play, responding to it with playfulness, invention and enthusiasm, with the aim of sustaining experiences of shared enjoyment, social communication and shared thinking in play.

Theodorou and Nind point out that these roles are informed by what is considered educational best practice in relation to pedagogical interactions and support for learning. The model is based on natural situations of learning, where the child and adult participate cooperatively within positive experiences of relationship. Terms that are often used to describe roles in these situations of learning include 'guided participation' and 'scaffolding', both of which suggest cooperation, creativity, transaction, adjustment and accommodation on the part of both adult and child. The adult seeks to understand what the child is bringing to the interaction in terms of understanding and ideas, and how they are experiencing the interaction emotionally. The adult continually monitors this and adjusts their own responses as a way of maximizing the child's pleasure in engagement and maintaining the interaction.

It is important to be clear how these roles and relationships in situations of learning differ from conceptualizations of adult-child relations that are often used in autism education. Many interventions used with autistic children describe the adult as 'instructing', 'eliciting' or 'prompting' the child, and as 'structuring' learning situations. These terms suggest much less emotional responsiveness on the part of the adult, less equality and cooperation within the child-adult relationship, and probably less meaningful learning experiences. There is less of a sense of teaching and learning as a collaborative enterprise that requires continual monitoring of children's experience on the part of the teacher. Figure 5.1 sets out some of the attributes that are required in an educational practitioner to be an effective play partner of children with autism.

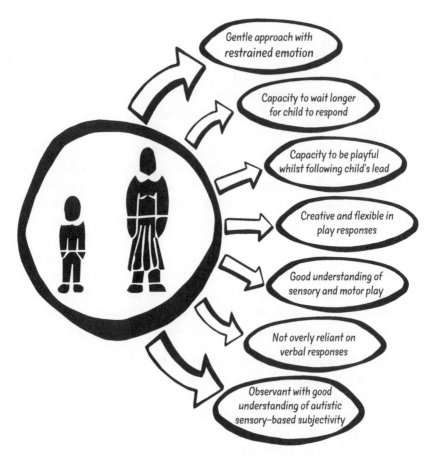

Figure 5.1 Capacities within the adult that make them effective play partners

Assessment for learning in relation to play

In order for teachers to be able to carry out these roles, it is important that they gain an understanding of the child's perspective in play and what meanings are being created by children within their play and playful interactions. The way in which teachers do this is known as assessment for learning or formative assessment. Assessment for learning stands in contrast to assessment *of* learning, or summative assessment, which is more of a formal testing of pupils' skills and knowledge. Assessment for learning is a less formal approach to assessment and is an integral part of everyday classroom practice. A large part of what teachers do involves assessment for learning, where they take steps to find out about children's experiences of learning contexts and what they understand. The purpose of this is for teachers to know how to plan learning that is interesting and accessible to children and results in higher levels of achievement. Teachers spend time observing pupils, asking them questions and reflecting on their learning experiences. They do this with sensitivity, having first developed supportive and trusting relationships with pupils.

Assessment of children's play is a crucial part of what teachers and other educational practitioners do to support children's learning, particularly in the early years. Play is a rich context for learning, but it is not one about which adults have a clear understanding. Teachers need to make extensive use of observation and talking to children to find out what play means for them, and what interests, ideas, skills and concerns children are bringing to their play. Teachers use this information to inform their practice and plan how to move children on in their learning. In this way they are able to plan for new learning contexts, introduce new play materials and develop the play space. They are also informed about their own roles – as play supporter, mediator and play partner – and provided with ideas about what they might say and do and what they may need to address in a child's behaviour.

In carrying out assessments of children's play, teachers and other educational practitioners document what children do by writing descriptions, taking photographs and collecting samples of children's play products. They do this to support conversations they have with children about their play, but also to facilitate children's own reflection on their learning. Pupil reflection on processes of learning is thought to be one of the most powerful ways in which new learning is achieved, and part of the reason that assessment for learning and other methods in reflective teaching are believed to have the most impact on children as learners. Much more information about assessment for learning is provided in a companion volume in this series, *Observation, Assessment and Planning in Inclusive Autism Education*. Set out ahead is an overview of the process of assessment for learning with particular reference to children's play.

Making observations

Teachers understand that an important part of educational practice concerns taking time to observe what children do. Much of the time these observations are not planned and occur as a result of the teacher noticing an idea, behaviour, activity or conversation that seems especially relevant to a child's learning. They may write down what happened or take a photograph, or ask questions for further clarification. Teachers may note children's actions and responses to a situation, including emotional responses, and their comments or ideas. Importantly, non-verbal information about behaviour, including facial expression, use of body, sound, gesture and orientation, will be seen as offering valuable insight into the child's experience of learning contexts and what meanings they are creating.

Information about naturally occurring learning is gathered in this way and may be used to inform further investigation. Observation may be carried out in a more planned way thereafter, looking at a specific play activity, time of the day, location or relationship. Information may be gathered more systematically to gain an overall 'picture' of patterns of play experience and interaction in order to assess what is being learned. Table 5.1 sets out methods of observation that can be used to investigate children's play, with the relative strengths and limitations of each method also described.

Table 5.1 Methods for educational observation

Method of observation	Purpose	Method of recording	Benefits/limitations
Participant observation	A naturalistic form of observation which takes place as part of ongoing practice. Can be planned ahead of time or happen spontaneously, but does not intrude on children's naturally occurring activity. Used to record patterns of behaviour that are identified as significant.	Informal narrative account, written up quickly as notes during an observation or immediately afterwards. May be supplemented with photographs or video footage, which can also be annotated.	Benefits: Good at capturing the quality of natural situations of play and requires no advance preparation. Limitations: Relies on observer remembering small details of children's behaviour and interactions, and can result in large amounts of information being recorded.
Ecological observation	Note is made of who begins a playful interaction, who else gets involved and how play unfolds. Can be used to record children's social play or play with the physical environment. Similar in structure to the play cycle.	Records sequence of actions, roles and comments of all those involved in a group play situation. Records roles in relation to: participating, facilitating, directing, resisting and eavesdropping.	Benefits: Views child as part of a group and play as an unfolding process. Captures roles within play and the dynamics of relationships. Limitations: Preliminary investigation may be needed to establish significant members of a child's peer group as a way of knowing who to observe.

Method of observation	Purpose	Method of recording	Benefits/limitations
Event sampling	Focused investigation of an event that has been identified as a significant influence on play behaviour. Events may be 'positive' and involve optimum engagement, or may involve difficulty, anxiety and conflict.	Formal recording of an event using a schedule. Schedules used to record a series of similar events, duration, who is involved and what happened.	Benefits: Events that are similar can be compared over time and may serve as evidence of learning and development. Limitations: Observer needs to be present when event occurs, or practitioners need to share responsibility for observing.
Time sampling	Notes the frequency of a behaviour within a time period. Can be used only for behaviour that is clearly defined and observable.	Behaviour is recorded when it occurs or if it occurs during an interval of observation. Behaviour needs to be defined beforehand and a formal system of recording used to ensure accuracy.	Benefits: Provides measurable information about social behaviour – that is, how often it occurs or if it occurs at all. Limitations: The experiences of autistic children are not always processed in the same time frame as non-autistic children.
Mapping	Maps a child's use of the play space. Indicates children's preferences in play and where they feel comfortable. When used at different time intervals, records change and play development. Can be used to map two children's activity as a way of exploring the nature of their relationship.	A map is drawn of the playground, classroom play area or other significant space. Where children go, for how long, in what sequence and who they meet are recorded on the map as arrows, names and numbers.	Benefits: Focuses on an important area of assessment for autistic children – that is, their response to the environment – and may provide useful information about emotional well-being. Limitations: Does not describe quality of play.

Listening to children

Listening to children and asking them questions are part of observation-led pedagogy. It is possible to have conversations with children about what they are doing as a way of providing more detailed information and to clarify what you have observed. Talking to children, and to adults who know them, including their parents and other professionals, helps educational practitioners gain a better understanding of children's perspective and what sense they are making of a situation. This is especially relevant to play, which may require more in the way of adults having to interpret children's behaviour and the influences and ideas that support it.

Children can be asked questions informally during an observation – for example, the name of a game, what actions they are performing or what one child said to another. Alternatively, children can be asked questions about their play outside of the play situation. For autistic children, it is useful to base questions on visual images, showing a photograph of a game that a child particularly enjoys and asking specific questions about this. You may ask children to describe a game, who plays and what happens in the game, perhaps sequencing a series of photographs. Language should be kept simple, and conversations should always be based on specific real-life events. More general questions about play, such as 'What do you like to play?' or 'Who do you play with?', may lead some autistic children to interpret this in the light of where they are or who they are with at the time the question is asked, rather than their general experience of play and friendship. Sometimes it is helpful to ask questions in situ – that is, where a game or activity actually takes place – so that children can act out their play and actual play objects can be referred to. Table 5.2 sets out simple questions for conversations with children about their play and friendship.

Recording information

The process of observing and listening to children within assessment for learning is intimately bound up with that of recording their play activity. Recording can take a variety of forms, from making quickly jotted notes during an activity or writing down key words to be written up as a fuller account after an activity has come to an end to more formal and systematic methods of recording. The way in which an observation is carried out will determine the method of recording (see Table 5.1), but taking photographs and video, writing down snippets of dialogue and storing the products of children's play can accompany observations.

The purpose of recording children's play is to collect evidence of their learning and as a method of supporting further learning. Documented play makes the process of playing visible to both adults and children, and information and images can be used in conversations with children about their play. Talking to children about their play experience enables them to reflect on their learning through play

Table 5.2 Simple questions to ask children about their play and friendships

Looking at photographs of children's favourite games and play activities	Describe ___ *(naming a game)* What happens first in ___? What happens next? What is ___ doing? *(pointing at a peer)* What is ___ saying? Who is the leader?
Looking at photographs of peers	Describe ___ What games do you like to play with ___? What do you like about ___? Is there anything you don't like? Who is funny? What do they do? *(choosing from photos)* Who makes you laugh? Who do you understand? Who don't you understand?
Asking questions in situ and handling play objects	What do you like? What do you not like? What's your favourite thing to do here? What's your second favourite? Show me what you do with this. What do you look for here?
Touring the playground	What do you do here? Show me what you do here. Where do you go? Where do you not go? Where is the best place to be by yourself? Where is the best place to be with others/watch others? What do you like in the playground?
Asking children questions in friendship groups	Describe ___ *(pointing to a peer)* What do you like about ___? When do you play together? What's your favourite game? What's your second favourite? Third? What do you talk about? Who speaks and who listens? How does s/he make you laugh? When do you fall out? What do you do next?

and supports understanding and the consolidation of knowledge. Reflection is thought to be an essential learning process for all children, and for children with autism reflecting on situations of play can be especially important as a way of furthering social understanding and providing social explanation.

One educational method used for the purpose of assessment and recording is that of Learning Stories (Carr and Lee, 2012). These are descriptive records of key moments of learning which record the cognitive, social, emotional and physical processes involved in clear and visual ways. Writing Learning Stories serves the purpose of making hidden learning processes much more visible and understandable to children, including children with autism. Reading through stories about play can support the development of a clearer understanding of a play situation and what everyday practices and norms are operating. This supports all children's participation since the understanding and cooperativeness of peers can be developed in this way too. Box 5.1 sets out the process of writing a Learning Story and provides an example.

Box 5.1 Learning Stories

Learning Stories were developed by Margaret Carr and Wendy Lee (2012) as a form of practice in assessment for learning. A Learning Story is a narrative description of a child or group of children in a critical moment of learning. It is the teacher who identifies this, having first noticed something significant in children's behaviour and recorded the details. A Learning Story always takes the form of a narrative since this is thought to be the best method of capturing the complexity of learning and the interconnectedness of cognitive, social, emotional and bodily processes. It describes the child in the third person as a way of giving a story-like quality to the event and making it more shareable with children. For this reason too, a Learning Story is always accompanied by at least one picture, either a photograph or children's drawing, and should be highly visual in nature.

Learning Stories are for the purpose of teacher reflection on processes of learning, and for documenting and profiling children's attainments. However, they also allow children to reflect on their learning experiences, helping them understand how they took an interest in something, became involved, explored an idea or feeling or shared another person's ideas. In this way, what the child has done is made more visible to them and consolidates learning. They can be supported to gain a better understanding of the skills that were used, roles that were adopted and interactions that took place, and so be enriched in terms of their experience.

A story should describe a sequence of events, but it should also explain in child-friendly terms what these events mean in terms of a child's learning. A story should also outline learning the teacher might plan for next. Learning Stories concern positive experiences of engagement as a way of maximizing children's investment in and openness to reflection. They may be constructed in collaboration with other adults – for example, parents, other practitioners and outside agencies – who might contribute to the interpretation of what the recorded event means for a child. They can also be written in collaboration with children, who might suggest the title or ideas for design and provide some of the visual detail. The example provided here concerns a story about an autistic child, Charlie, aged 7, who is learning to join in with other children's non-verbal games.

Example of a Learning Story
Charlie joins in with children's games

Charlie likes to play by himself. When he plays by himself, he imagines that he is shooting aliens and fighting baddies.

Charlie is sometimes interested in other children, especially Jake, Sammy and Lola. Charlie is learning to play their games and likes it when they play ninjas, and creep and crawl around the playground. He also joins in when they play chase and the game of hide-and-seek. Charlie is learning to look at other children when they play these games. He watches them when they run around and follows them where they go. He enjoys doing this and laughs and smiles when he plays with his friends.

Next steps in learning:
Charlie can also join in with Sammy and Lola's game of cats, which involves moving like a cat and pretending to be a cat family.

Investigating children's unique play cultures

In investigating children's play, it is vitally important to collect *specific* pieces of information. It is not enough to observe that a child played with a group of children at break time or that they seem to have a friend. It is important to record with whom they play, noting names, and what particular games they enjoy and how they play them, along with the quality of any playful interaction. Children have different play preferences and engage in different types of play; however, the games they play are played repeatedly, over weeks, months and even years. It is worthwhile finding out about the nature of play for particular groups of children and about favourite games. An important point made by Corsaro and Johannesen (2007) is that children use their personal interests, concerns and knowledge of the world to create *unique* play cultures, which are shared within their peer group. Different groups of children may play similar games in different settings, but the meaning of the play, the details of the games, the patterns of interaction and the dynamics of relationships will be specific within particular settings and for individual peer groups.

In making assessments of children's play, it is necessary to find out about the unique play cultures that exist for them. For a child with autism, this provides information about how appropriate their participation is in social processes in their setting and how peers perceive them. Social competency is not something that is free-floating, but exists within actual social relations. Adults need to be careful not to make assumptions about the nature of social relationships for children. A child with autism who is focused on a particular computer game, for example, and who talks only about this, may be perceived as competent within a group of children who also have an interest in that game. The child may be perceived as highly competent if their knowledge of the game is greater than that of their peers. Conversely, where the play culture in a setting is not that focused on computer games or where other children have equal knowledge, the child with autism may be judged as weak in terms of their social competency and viewed by other children as 'different', 'odd' and 'boring'.

Play, interaction and friendship

Approaches to educating children with autism often separate out social interaction, play and friendship as if they are somehow distinct areas of functioning, but studies of childhood and children's everyday lives show us that these things are not experienced as separate entities by children themselves. Children measure the qualities of their friendships by the amount of enjoyment they derive in playing with someone, and playfulness often defines children's social interactions. Friendship and experiences of close relationships support the development of social understanding and promote competencies in social interaction, whilst increasing sophistication in play requires increasing capacities in social communication, coordinated behaviour and a shared sense of purpose.

Investigation of children's experiences of play should be seen, therefore, as engagement with the details of play, but also with the ways in which children interact with each other and their experiences of friendship. Patterns of interaction and forms of friendship, moreover, should be seen as existing in different ways for different children – for example, involving high or low levels of talk, high or low levels of physical activity, of competitiveness, of 'silly behaviour' (as perceived by others) and so on. Information about all areas of functioning will contribute to an understanding of the unique influences on children's play cultures in your setting, how play, interaction and friendship are experienced for particular children, and whether learning and development are occurring.

Social roles in play and friendship

It is important not to impose adult assumptions and values when investigating children's play cultures. For example, adults may believe that children should have equal roles in play and an equality of partnership in friendships. There may be an assumption that members of a group should have equal voice and should equally be heard, and when this is found not to be the case, to deem it a problem. This does not necessarily reflect how children experience social roles in relation to friendship and play, however, which very often are organized along the lines of leaders and followers. Some children's games depend on children having unequal roles and non-reciprocal turns, and some children are skilled at taking a dominant role without this leading to undue conflict within the group. Others may be happy for someone else to take the lead, especially those who do not have many play ideas to contribute. Inequality in play can sometimes be a problem – for example, one child always being assigned a role they do not want in play (e.g. the baddie) or another child who wants to be heard not being listened to, but it is important to know that inequality can also sustain playing and be something that children enjoy. This makes the quality of children's emotional involvement in play a particularly key area for investigation.

Dominant, peer group and individual play cultures

Investigating unique play cultures and the dynamics of social relationships is aided by thinking in terms of the differing cultures that exist for children within one setting and the ways in which these exert influences – positive or negative – on the activity of individual children. It is possible to identify culture at three levels:

1   *The dominant culture of the larger group* – this may be a class, year group or key stage. This will be influenced by the make-up of the group and such

factors as age, gender, class and ethnicity, but also factors such as the general level of awareness and acceptance of difference and diversity. Groups of children can be defined in terms of their attitudes, interests and behaviours – for example, levels of competitiveness, tolerance, conflict and supportiveness. Levels of physical activity, modes of communication, cultural interests, and play and interaction preferences are further considerations. Some settings are defined by the homogeneity of groups (members of groups are similar to each other) or by the existence of mixed groups of children – for example, that girls are friends with boys or that children who are 'different' are not excluded. Knowledge of all these areas is important as a way of understanding how easily individuals are able to 'fit in' with the socioculture of their setting.

2   *Smaller peer groups* – these are formed when children associate regularly, seek each other out to play with and especially enjoy each other's company. Smaller peer groups share interests, understandings, attitudes, values and concerns, and use these in their interactions with each other. For some peer groups, these will be strongly aligned with the dominant culture that exists in their setting – a group of boys who play football regularly, for example, being one of many such groups on the playground. For others, their group may exist 'outside' of the dominant culture and be perceived by others, children and adults, as quirky, different or 'naughty'. A group of boys may be perceived as unusually rough or loud in their play, for example, and other groups as particularly kind and mature, or alternatively talkative and 'silly'.

3   *The individual child* – very often children with autism have a small peer group, which consists of perhaps one, two or three children who share an interest and level of social competency. However, their play activity may also exist outside of any social context and may need to be described in individualistic terms. Children with autism play partly in social ways, but also non-socially, engaging with sensory, perceptual and motor play with objects and the environment in ways that cannot be socially shared. They may also engage playfully with other people who they experience not interpersonally but more as sensory objects – for example, wanting to play with someone's hair. Investigation is then of a play culture of one, looking at how it is experienced by the child and what meanings they are creating, though it is also possible to explore how this 'culture of one' is perceived by other children, who accepts it and who tries to engage with it.

Figure 5.2 provides ideas for lines of enquiry when investigating the socioculture that exists for groups and individual children. What is of interest is not only the culture that is being used and produced by children but also where it is shared. This provides information for planning learning opportunities for further social sharing and to support children's ongoing social development.

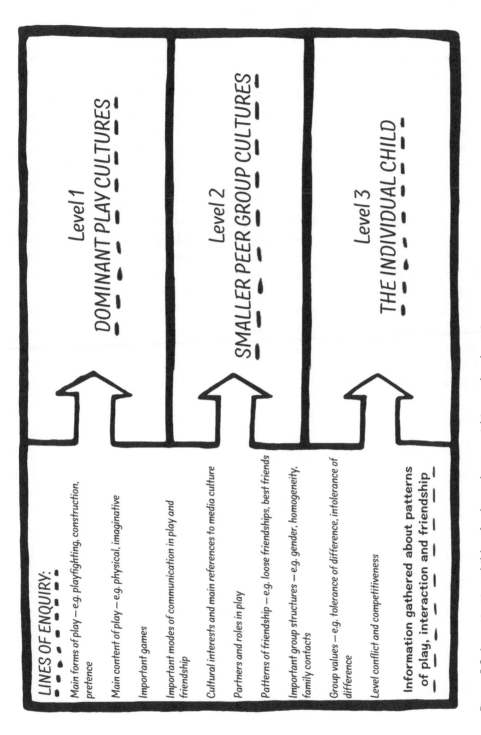

LINES OF ENQUIRY:

Main forms of play – e.g. playfighting, construction, pretence

Main content of play – e.g. physical, imaginative

Important games

Important modes of communication in play and friendship

Cultural interests and main references to media culture

Partners and roles in play

Patterns of friendship – e.g. loose friendships, best friends

Important group structures – e.g. gender, homogeneity, family contacts

Group values – e.g. tolerance of difference, intolerance of difference

Level conflict and competitiveness

Information gathered about patterns of play, interaction and friendship

Level 1
DOMINANT PLAY CULTURES

Level 2
SMALLER PEER GROUP CULTURES

Level 3
THE INDIVIDUAL CHILD

Figure 5.2 Investigating children's play cultures within a school setting

Assessing sensory play

Given the importance of sensory-based experience for people with autism, children's sensory experience of play is a key area of assessment in inclusive autism education. Sensory play involves playing with the properties of objects without applying any social meanings. In sensory play, a child may enjoyably engage with reflected light or the movement and flow of objects, but without connecting this emotional experience to any social experience, social role or their experience of relationships. Many children engage in sensory play, but non-autistic children will make more social meanings within their sensory play. Teachers and other educational practitioners need to be able to recognize sensory play in the myriad ways in which it manifests in children's activity. The characteristics of play behaviour will be present – namely, absorption, pleasure, creativity and spontaneity – but the quality of play experience will be sensory-based. Table 5.3 sets out frequent focal points for children in sensory play. These constitute forms of engagement which you need to be able to recognize in children's play behaviour, particularly that of children with autism.

Assessment of sensory play involves the same processes of observing, conversations with adults and children and recording information. A record can be made of children's sensory engagement, what they enjoy and seek out in sensory experience, but also what frightens them or makes them anxious (see Figure 5.3). Assessment of children's sensory responses to toys, everyday objects and the environment helps

Table 5.3 Focal points of sensory play

Shape	*Interest in:* • straight lines • curves • corners and edges • flatness • gaps and holes • protrusions
Light	*Interest in:* • quality of light – e.g. soft, glowing • patterns and contrast in light • on/off light, flashing light • reflected light • colour and light • movement and light
Movement	*Interest in:* • appearance and disappearance of objects • objects that flow • objects going round and round • erratic movement – e.g. jitter balls, hoover – may be experienced as frightening • perspective – e.g. lining up objects near and far

Colour	Interest in:
	• 'pops' of colour – e.g. one colour that contrasts against a background
	• pattern and colour
	• coloured light
	• coloured fabric
	• looking through colour – e.g. through coloured plastic
Engagement of the senses	• sight
	• sound
	• touch
	• taste/smell
	• body sense – e.g. the body in space, movement, being held

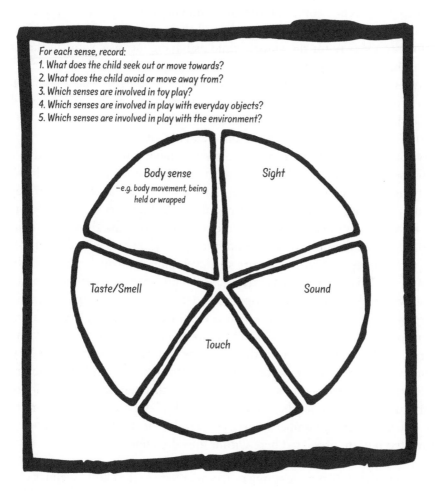

Figure 5.3 Assessment of sensory play

support practitioner planning for learning contexts and for developing the play space appropriately.

Curricular aims through play-based learning

For typically developing children, play supports learning and development across a number of domains: cognitive, social, communicative, linguistic and physical. It also has intrinsic value in that it supports emotional well-being, a healthy sense of self and feelings of safety, happiness and confidence. For children with autism, whose development is atypical, the role of play in learning and development is less certain. There is a belief by some theorists and practitioners that learning through play does not occur for children with autism and that it serves no purpose to support the development of children's play. From watching autistic children play, however, it is apparent that they also experience absorption and pleasure in play activity, which may be predominantly concerned with playing with the sensory properties of objects, people and the environment. They also derive positive experiences from this and invest themselves and their play ideas. It stands to reason, therefore, to see play for the autistic child as having intrinsic value in that it produces feelings of safety, happiness and well-being, and as a form of leisure and self-expression, where the self being expressed is an autistic one. Having autism means experiencing higher levels of stress as a result of sensory processing difficulties and the greater demands of being in a social environment, and play offers an important space for relaxation and non-social activity.

Play for children with autism is also seen as having instrumental value and is widely used to support the development of social communication, children's play activity used as a platform for gentle experiences of social sharing. In developmental approaches to autism, children's play-based activity is used as a starting point for engaging them in social interaction and providing them with enjoyable experiences of communicating with another person. Figure 5.4 sets out a framework that conceptualizes the nature of development through play for children with autism. This suggests as a starting point children's sensory-based non-social play activity and maps out a developmental pathway that encompasses early experiences of social sharing in play which is child-led and usually involves an adult as play partner, and later experiences of peer play and friendships with other children. Within the framework, the experience of play is envisaged as 'atypical' throughout, in that sensory, perceptual and motor features of play and interaction remain strong influences on children's behaviour throughout their development.

Curricular aims that can be achieved through play-based learning for children with autism concern a number of areas of development, all of which are strongly interrelated but are presented here within four domains:

1   *emotional well-being* – learning outcomes relate to the child's feelings of safety, security and happiness within the school setting, enjoyment of special interests

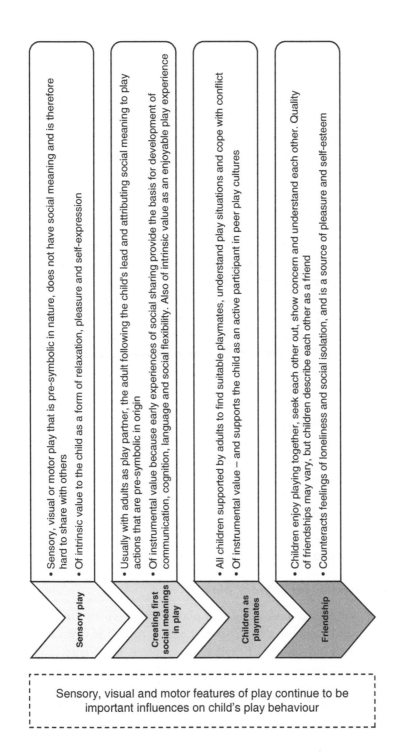

Figure 5.4 Play development for children with autism within an inclusive setting (adapted from Conn, 2014)

and strengths, developing awareness of self and capacity for self-expression, and developing ability to regulate their own feelings;

2   *social participation* – learning outcomes relate to the child's developing capacity to participate in child-led one-to-one interactions with an adult play partner, developing capacity to participate in enjoyable play interactions with other children that are supported by an adult, developing interest in and ability to follow other people's ideas and to contribute flexibly ideas of their own. Learning outcomes in relation to this area of development also concern developing strategies for dealing with conflict and emotionally challenging social experiences (e.g. having to wait your turn);

3   *communication* – learning outcomes relate to the child's understanding and responding to non-verbal and verbal communication and enjoyment of communicative experiences, as well as increasing resourcefulness, flexibility and confidence in relation to communication;

4   *making sense of the world* – learning outcomes relate to the child's developing capacity to recognize and respond to ideas and social concepts and to use socially based strategies to make sense of the world. Learning outcomes also relate to the child's ability to make connections between two or more ideas or experiences, developing socially meaningful sequences of actions and events and adopting socially recognizable roles and relationships.

It is possible to see from these aims that learning through play for children with autism serves a similar purpose as it does for all children. Engaging in play is an important way in which children engage with others and make sense of the world, both social and non-social, and also has value as a form of self-expression, relaxation and leisure. In schools, we need to recognize children's play in all its forms and plan play contexts that support the full range of curricular aims.

Developing inclusive play contexts

Selecting materials for sensory play

Sensory play is the most natural form of playful engagement for autistic children, and the selection of play materials should reflect this. It is often in sensory play that children with autism are at their most creative, most entertained and least anxious. Toys that are appropriate for sensory play are ones that are interesting in terms of their shape, movement, colour, light, texture and smell. Toys that make appealing sounds, reflect light and have interesting moving parts and pleasant textures will be important, as will play items that swing, rock, bounce, spin and provide children with an enjoyable experience of bodily self. Since manufactured toys are often not designed for their sensory qualities, but rather for their interactive and pretend purposes, it is helpful to think in terms of non-toy items too.

Everyday objects and ordinary household items can have great potential for creativity in sensory play, and it is a good idea to think imaginatively and cast your
net widely when resourcing children's play. Box 5.2 suggests small- and large-scale
items that may support children's sensory play. A number of online commercial
enterprises that specifically focus on sensory play have become established over
the years, and these provide further ideas about materials to use for sensory play.
Natural objects can also be a useful source of play materials since they do not have
the social world imprinted on them and do not dictate how something is used in
play. Natural objects also lend themselves to play that involves collecting things,
organizing, arranging and matching, and other forms of visual play enjoyed by
some children with autism.

Box 5.2   Sensory play materials

Small-scale materials

Bubbles
Spotlights and torches
Mood lamps
Mirrors and reflecting objects
Shiny objects – e.g. costume jewellery
Ribbons and streamers
Jack-in-the-box toys
Lego® and other construction blocks
Marble runs
Play goo
Ooze tubes
Sand trays
Rice tables
Jigsaws and block puzzles
Collapsible spheres
Balls – e.g. koosh balls, wiggle balls
Sound toys
Toys with wheels
Train toys – e.g. Thomas the Tank Engine
Spinning toys
Flap-books and texture books
First 100 Words books, picture encyclopaedia and compendiums
Natural objects – e.g. to create series of things, patterns, for stacking

---

Large-scale materials

Swings
Slides
Trampoline
Spinning, swinging and rocking chairs
Rocking horse
Cushions
Parachute
Ball pool
Toys which children can ride on together: bicycles, toy tractors and so forth
Lycra cloth
Fabric – e.g. of different colours, with sparkly decoration
Lairs and dens
Tubes (for looking through)
Tunnels
Sandpit
Paddling pool

Selecting materials for pretend play

Making real items available for the creation of lifelike routines may support children's experience of pretend play – for example, providing real exercise books,
textbooks and equipment to play schools, or real kitchen tools and household
appliances for play in the home corner. Toys might be selected for their lifelike
quality and how accurately they represent the real-life equivalent. An important
feature of pretend play for an autistic child might be making models that have
realistic details and an intricate visual design, and interesting materials can be provided for this. Adults might also need to adjust their expectations about children's
play and not see model making as simply a precursor to the main event of children
acting out a pretend play narrative. Though some children with autism may be
interested in producing play narratives, for others the making or arranging of play
items may itself constitute the important experience of imaginative play.

Developing the play space

Just as the sensory qualities of play materials need consideration, so the play space
should be thought about in terms of its sensory features. Think about adding 'sensory spaces', where children can hide, be enfolded, go under, look through and
feel. Play spaces that are strongly visual and have predictable features can provide
a secure and enjoyable environment. Lines on the ground, railings of a fence or a

series of windows can be part of a child's play environment and areas to consider in terms of development – for example, attaching things to a fence or arranging items in windows.

Groups of children actively playing is sometimes an overwhelming experience for children with autism, and you might need to consider adding spaces that are slightly to one side or slightly hidden. Consider developing spaces where children can watch others in play, which is something that children with autism often like to do. Spaces above the play space can be useful for this purpose. Making use of natural spaces to play also provides a welcome relief from the demands of social space and results in more engagement, relaxation and enjoyment for children (see Box 5.3).

Some children may benefit from having the play space clearly defined. It is possible to map out for a child the key areas of a specific game on a piece of paper or as a tour of the play space. As with other forms of learning support, strategies to support play need to be tailored to the particular games and features of play that exist in your setting. You will have gathered information about these from your investigations of children's play and can use this as the basis for explanations to children about play narratives, roles, expectations and use of the play space.

Box 5.3 Natural playgrounds

Within education there has been recent focus on learning spaces and the relationship between place and children's ability to learn. Increasingly, the classroom is seen as only one place in which learning occurs, and perhaps not always the most effective place for learning. Learning outside the classroom, in outdoor classrooms, natural spaces and alternative learning environments, is viewed as an approach to enriching children's engagement with their learning and raising achievement.

For pupils with autism, natural spaces that are removed from the demands of social space may be more comfortable and accessible as learning environments. Many people with autism describe being in nature and amongst plants and wildlife as a preferable experience to being with people and in places created by people. The sensory experience of nature is different, and there will be less in the way of social noise, language and communication, providing perhaps a greater sense of calm, relaxation and 'centeredness'. The importance of children's engagement with their learning, and centrality of self-experience in this, means that natural learning spaces may provide a more compelling learning environment for an autistic child, where barriers to learning are removed, such as social stress, anxiety, rigidity, needing to control learning situations, and inability to focus or attend.

A natural playground consists of features such as trees and other living plants, natural surfaces and landscapes, and natural elements such as water, soil and sand. The use of manufactured play items, both large and small, is kept to a minimum, and there is an emphasis on the use of natural objects and materials as play items. The sensory features of the natural world – smells, sounds, textures, viewpoints and things to observe – are key elements of children's experience, with teacher planning involving finding ways in which these can be developed. The social expectations of natural playgrounds are characterised by a child-centred approach to interaction and learning, with greater freedom allowed for children's personal interests, activity, movement and exploration.

Whilst natural playgrounds are seen as an important time away from social space for autistic children, social interaction and social learning through play may also be a feature. Children's engagement with other people, adults and children, may be mediated through natural resources and nature-based activities. Making collections of natural objects, sorting, stacking and arranging natural items, digging, building and exploring are activities that can be shared in natural playgrounds.

In making assessments of children's activity in natural playgrounds, Waite and Pratt's (2011) planning framework supports reflection on how place supports learning. They ask:

- what might the place mean for the child?
- what valuable learning might therefore take place?
- how does this relate to curricular priorities in the setting or nationally?

Supporting the development of social play

Children's play may be sensory-based or only minimally socially interactive, but can nevertheless provide a rich platform for social learning. Part of the challenge of play-based learning in inclusive autism education is for teachers to find ways of producing socially shareable, 'symbolic' meaning out of a child's sensory-based, pre-symbolic play experience. In order to achieve this, teachers must support the child in deriving enjoyment from a shared play space and social reward in interactively playing with others. For children who are playing in mostly non-social ways, this will probably involve the teacher, support worker or parent being their first play partner, playing alongside and carefully following the child's lead with a high degree of sensitivity to their emotional response to social engagement. For children who are more socially oriented in their play, support may be provided in the form of helping them to find suitable playmates, mediating peer interactions in play and helping children establish friendships.

Adults as play partners

Play is often used as a platform for the development of social communication in children with autism, adults as play partners actively seeking to engage them in brief but enjoyable experiences of social interaction. Support for early playful experiences of social communication is seen as a way of developing a child's sense of relatedness to another human being and of shared communication, and forms the basis of many developmental approaches to autism (see e.g. Greenspan and Wieder, 2006; Nind and Hewett, 2005; Prizant et al., 2006; Seach, 2007). Common to these approaches is the model of preverbal interaction that exists for typically developing young children, where the parent and young child engage in intense, highly pleasurable and repeated experiences of meaningful interaction and social communication. In these early interactions, the parent is attuned to the young child's experience and tries to find ways of interacting that are mutually enjoyable, carefully monitoring the emotional quality of the interaction to ensure that the child does not feel overwhelmed and withdraw.

For children with autism, experiences of interactive play are thought to support the development of social attention, and in turn of cognition, communication, language and social flexibility. In play, the play partner follows the child's lead and play interests, but seeks out ways of creating socially shareable, symbolic meanings around these. They may attribute social meaning to play actions even when none exist for the autistic child. For example, they may say 'Bye-bye' when an object disappears or provide real-life sound effects to accompany the child's actions with an object. They may add their social interest too, observing and mirroring actions or commenting on the play using modified language. In this way, a child can be encouraged to notice the play partner and occasionally make reference to them for meaning. Children can be provided with brief but important episodes of joint attention, coordinated action, turn taking and reciprocal communication that give them pleasure and provide a sense of well-being in relation to the presence of another person.

Inevitably, these kinds of interaction are most often found within child-adult situations of play. The level of support for communication that is needed and degree of social attunement on the part of the play partner are something that an adult is more likely to achieve. The adult as play partner must make careful observation of the child in play and find creative ways of engaging their social interest. They must show resilience in the face of play withdrawal and be alert to opportunities for interactive engagement and meaningful communication. Table 5.4 describes some of the ways in which an adult play partner produces social meaning in play.

Table 5.4 Ways adults share social meaning with children in play

Add social interest	• observe • stay focused – maintain an observational state of mind • share attention – following the child's lead • notice and name objects • differentiate one thing from another – e.g. 'Big wheels, small wheels'.
Add language	• provide a running commentary on the child's play activity • add language to play actions – e.g. 'Gone!', 'Bye-bye', 'Hello!' • introduce 'scripts' for playful interaction – e.g. 'Ready, steady, go', 'Again!' • speak in the third person using modified language and a gentle voice • keep emotional expression restrained so as not to overwhelm the child
Add music	• speak in a sing-song voice • use a musical accompaniment for play or as a substitute for 'talk' • add sound effects • use familiar songs, rhymes and jingles as 'borrowed language' • provide relaxing music to help children self-regulate
Add rhythm	• rock or swing child gently • imitate and mirror • repeat experiences and interactions • support child to bounce on a trampoline • use call and response and action rhymes

In many educational settings, this way of working is seen as an individual form of pedagogy, one that is provided as a unique programme for the learner and delivered alongside the core curriculum – for example, as learning opportunities arise within the normal flow of interaction or as a timetabled session that is additionally provided.

Helping children find playmates

Children with autism sometimes find it hard to work out who might be a good playmate or how to involve themselves in a game, but nevertheless show an interest in being with other children. Some children may need to be introduced to the children in their class through pictures, perhaps in the form of a photo album of classmates, with their names also clearly written. Face blindness is a part of autism for some individuals and means that a child may not easily be able to distinguish between the faces of their peers. Children can also feel overwhelmed by the sheer number in their group and find it hard to process movement, noise, talk and fast-paced interactions. Pointing out visual markers in relation to other children's appearance – for example, who has long hair, who always wears a headband or who is taller in the group – may help with recognizing others, and also reduce the degree of stress involved in peer interaction.

Identifying playmates for children involves thinking about who makes a good match in terms of play interests and modes of play communication. Children who are quiet may play well with a child who carries out play with low verbal content, or conversely with someone who likes to lead. Children who play in physical ways, who like running, climbing and playfighting, for example, might also make good playmates for a child who also likes doing these things, though conflict might eventually become an issue. Conflict between playmates should not be judged as a reason for children not to be encouraged to play together, however, since it is a natural part of play and something that supports social competency. Children who share similar levels of social competency and language ability often enjoy being play partners. It is possible to partner a child who is socially competent with a less able child, but be aware that this form of support is about one child adopting the role of 'little adult' and may not result in real friendship. Play supports the development of friendship, but friendship occurs where there is social parity and a sense of mutually enjoyed interaction. Children's personalities, attitudes and out-looks are important in thinking about playmates. Some children are bossy in their interactions and try to dominate their peers. Others may also organize peer inter-actions, but using a gentler style and with a greater sense of inclusiveness. Some children have more patience, some are more accepting of difference and some are simply happy to go along with others. All these influences need to be taken into consideration when reflecting on children's play experience and the provision of learning supports.

Supporting children as playmates may involve encouraging children to play alongside each other and share a play space. It may mean the adult also playing alongside, to model cooperative actions, suggest something for children to say or explain what is going on within the play. An adult can help sort out misunder-standings or conflict, and also praise children for playing well with each other. A non-autistic peer may be instructed simply to 'stay, play and talk' to another child and commended when they do this.

Friendship

Friendship for all children takes different forms, and adults should not assume that every child has a best friend or that friends always spend time talking to each other. Friendship can be a more transitory experience for children than it is for adults and more of an expression of closeness based on a particular game or a one-off event, such as a birthday party or outing. Some children have friendships that endure, but some never experience a close friendship. Having no friends does not necessarily mean that a child is isolated socially, however, and they may still be involved in peer activity and peer play. Girls tend to have different experiences of friendship to boys, having closer and tighter friendship groups with more declarations of emotional commitment. Friendship can also be influenced by factors other than gender, including a shared culture, familial networks and a shared level of social competency.

Judy Dunn (2004), who has written extensively about children's friendships, notes that friendship is marked out from ordinary acquaintance by the emotional quality involved and the degree to which children understand each other and show concern. Friends are more invested to overcome situations of conflict, though conflict is a natural part of friendship and something that helps children learn how to manage social relationships and their own feelings. Having fun is amongst criteria children use to identify someone who is a friend, though they might also cite the length of time they have known each other. Friends enjoy each other's company and mutually benefit from their interactions, sharing interests, values, experiences and skills.

Friendship and autism

A series of studies investigating the quality of friendship for autistic children found a mixed experience (Bauminger and Kasari, 2000; Calder et al., 2012; Chamberlain et al., 2007). Most autistic children are partly engaged in social networks and usually have at least one friend, though some have a wide social network and central status within a friendship group. Many children with autism make friends with children who are also experiencing some kind of social difficulty or who are outsiders to the group. The perception of what is a friend may be characteristically different for a child with autism, however. Typically developing children tend to perceive a friend as someone you play with and feel close to, but also as someone who is mentally present even when they are not there. Friendship for non-autistic children appears to have an internal dimension that counteracts a sense of loneliness with the knowledge that 'I am someone who has a friend'. Autistic children may experience feelings of loneliness, but the knowledge that they have a friend is not necessarily a defence against this. They might view the physical presence of another person as the only signifier of significant social contact. Conversely, they may feel that they are socializing and 'have friends' even when engaged in a solitary activity where other people are a background presence.

Supporting friendship

Some autistic children do not desire a friend, but others express feelings of loneliness and say they would like a friend. These children may not know how to go about establishing friendships and may not be particularly good at identifying someone who would make a good friend. An effective way of supporting friendship is to identify someone who might make a good friend and suggest enjoyable activities for children to do together. However, it may be important for adults to adjust their expectations about what is a friend since ordinary structures of friendship can operate slightly differently for children and young people with autism. Some children with autism do not recognize the social differences that exist between people, such as age, gender or race, as a barrier to friendship, though others might cite these things as an insurmountable obstacle to being with another person. Boys and girls may be more likely to be friends, and some children with autism may want only one friend, seeing close interaction with only one person as sufficient for their social needs. Sometimes these friendships have an intensity that is hard to support, but it is important not to judge this as a problem if both children demonstrate a satisfaction with an exclusive friendship. Some children prefer playing with younger children, whilst others seek out adults as friends, particularly ones with whom interaction is clear and conversation more enjoyable.

It is important to value friendship in all its forms and provide support in one or more of the following ways:

- help children to sort out their differences;
- provide a friendship group in which an adult supports enjoyable peer interactions (see Box 5.4);
- be an adult friend;
- put parents in touch so that meetings outside of school can be arranged.

Box 5.4   Friendship groups

A friendship group brings together children who are friends or who show an interest in becoming friends, or children adults think could be friends given some support. The group is for the purpose of bonding children's friendships through the provision of enjoyable experiences of being together. Friendship groups provide supported experiences of social interaction, where the adult facilitator helps children to create appropriate social responses and mediates peer interactions. Group aims might include developing children's interest in each other and willingness to engage, gaining a sense of enjoyment of being with others, sustaining social engagement for longer periods of time and developing children's capacity for recalling appropriate forms of social response. Further aims may address non-autistic peers' learning about and appreciation of autistic ways of interacting. These include giving people more time to respond, having a reduced expectation of eye contact and engaging in non-face-to-face conversation, and conversation without turn taking, where one person just listens whilst the other talks about their interests.

Children who are identified as friends or potential friends are invited to join a friendship group, the invitation couched in attractive terms. Ensure that group meetings do not encroach on another activity that group members enjoy. Organize a regular time and place, and ensure that these are consistent, always preparing the group beforehand for any change to routine. The same group of children should meet each time, and, for this reason, it is helpful to put a limit on the number of times a group meets to ensure that children do not feel they are missing out on something in class. Be sure to organize the group on the basis of friendship and not on children's learning needs. A child should not be invited to join the group if they have social needs but are not part of the peer group being offered support.

Make sure that friendship groups follow a predictable structure. Good practice involves repeating activities or games children especially enjoy and using simple rituals to begin and end sessions, such as a set greeting or ending routine. Activities should not rely too heavily on verbal communication. Within groups it is possible to provide children with ideas for their interactions, suggesting things to say, encouraging the use of a child's name to get their attention, encouraging children to wait a little longer for a response, and praising them for perseverance in communication. Children can be encouraged to notice something about another child's communication, and aspects of an interaction can be highlighted and explained. In this way, all group members, autistic and non-autistic, are supported to interact more effectively in their real-life interactions.

Friendship groups take a variety forms, including:

- using a game or activity that children already enjoy and providing this in a supported way within a group that meets regularly – for example, a lunchtime club based around a favourite board game, toy or computer programme;
- introducing children to new games that are particularly suited to their interests and social needs – for example, games that do not involve spoken language or are visually structured;
- providing fun activities that support the development of social communication – for example, circle games involving non-verbal communication and clear turn taking (see Table 5.5 for some ideas).

Table 5.5 Enjoyable games for friendship groups (adapted from Conn, 2007, and Conn, 2010)

1. Duck, duck, goose *A visually structured game*	Players sit in a circle whilst one player walks around the outside. This player touches other players on the shoulder, saying, 'Duck – duck – duck'. They choose one player to be 'It' by tapping that player and saying, 'Goose!' The first player runs round the circle and the 'goose' chases them. The first player tries to go all the way round the circle and sit in the empty space without being caught. If they do so, the game begins again.
2. Here is a beehive *Call and response that provides players with language for the game*	The adult slots their fingers together so that they are facing down and wriggling as if they are bees. The say these lines, performing accompanying actions with their hands: *Here is a beehive, but where are all the bees?* *They're hiding inside where nobody sees* *Here they come creeping, out of the door* *1–2–3–4* *Buzzzz (fingers wriggling out)* Actions to be performed include wiggling fingers to show the bees inside the hive, opening a door by opening out the thumbs, and counting out '1, 2, 3, 4' by joining each finger in turn – index, middle, ring and little finger – to form an arch. Children need to say only one line, '1–2–3–4', though they might like to join in with the 'Buzzz' as well.
3. Cars *A non-verbal communication game*	Players in pairs decide who is the driver and who is the car. The driver stands behind the car, both players facing in the same direction. The driver signals moves to the car: • resting the hand on the centre of the back of the car signals 'drive' • touching left/right shoulder signals 'turn' • removing hand signals 'stop'. Players drive round the play space, the driver ensuring the car does not 'crash' into objects or other people.
4. Letters of your name *A group coordination game*	Taking each group member in turn, call out the letters of their name in a call-and-response style. The group leader says a letter and the group repeats this back, with finally the whole name called out. Allow group members to take turns to be the caller and encourage group expression and rhythm around the call and response.

(Continued)

Table 5.5 (Continued)

5. Changing chairs
A group collaboration game

Chairs are set out randomly, not in a circle. Players sit in the chairs, with one player standing to one side of the group. One chair is left empty and the standing player tries to sit in it. They do this by walking towards the empty chair at a steady pace, making sure that they do not speed up. The other players try to prevent this player from sitting down by one player moving into the empty chair. As this player's chair becomes empty, the player who is 'on' changes direction and goes to sit in the vacated chair. The group continues to move into empty chairs as they become available, trying to prevent the player who is 'on' from sitting down. When this player eventually manages to sit down, another player is on.

References

Axline, V. M. (1964) *Dibs: In Search of Self*, London: Penguin Books.

Bagatell, N. (2010) 'From cure to community: transforming notions of autism', *Ethos*, 38: 33–55.

Baron-Cohen, S. (1987) 'Autism and symbolic play', *British Journal of Developmental Psychology*, 5: 139–48.

Bateson, G. (1972) *Steps to an Ecology of Mind*, London, Toronto, Sydney and New York: Granada Publishing.

Bauminger, N. and Kasari, C. (2000) 'Loneliness and friendship in high-functioning children with autism', *Child Development*, 71: 447–56.

Berger, D. S. (2002) *Music Therapy, Sensory Integration and the Autistic Child*, London and Philadelphia: Jessica Kingsley Publishers.

Bertram, T. and Pascal, C. (2002) *Effective Early Learning Programme Child Involvement Scale*, University College of Worcester, St Thomas Centre, Birmingham. Online: http://www.littlestarnursery.co.uk/wp-content/uploads/2014/05/leuven-scales.pdf (accessed 13 October 2014).

Billington, T. (2006) 'Working with autistic children and young people: sense, experience and the challenges for services, policies and practices', *Disability and Society*, 21: 1–13.

Blackman, L. (2009) *Lucy's Story: Autism and Other Adventures*, London and Philadelphia: Jessica Kingsley Publishers.

Bogdashina, O. (2003) *Sensory Perceptual Issues in Autism and Asperger Syndrome*, London and Philadelphia: Jessica Kingsley Publishers.

Brody, V. (1997) *The Dialogue of Touch: Developmental Play Therapy*, Northvale, NJ and London: Jason Aronson Inc.

Bundy, A. C. (1997) *Test of Playfulness (ToP) Manual, Version 3.4*, Ft. Collins: Colorado State University.

Burghardt, G. M. (2005) *The Genesis of Animal Play: Testing the Limits*, Cambridge, MA: MIT Press.

Burghardt, G. M. (2011) 'Defining and recognizing play', in A. Pellegrini (ed.) *Oxford Handbook of the Development of Play*, New York and London: Oxford University Press, 9–18.

Burn, A. (2013) 'Computer games on the playground: ludic systems, dramatised narrative and virtual embodiment', in R. Willett, C. Richards, J. Marsh, A. Burn and J. C. Bishop (eds.) *Children, Media and Playground Cultures: Ethnographic Studies of School Playtimes*, Basingstoke: Palgrave Macmillan, 120–44.

Caillois, R. (1958/2001) *Man, Play and Games*, Urbana and Chicago: University of Illinois Press.

Calder, L., Hill, V. and Pellicano, E. (2012) ' "Sometimes I want to play by myself": understanding what friendship means to children with autism in mainstream primary schools', *Autism*, 17: 296–316.

Carr, M. and Lee, W. (2012) *Learning Stories: Constructing Learner Identities in Early Education*, London, Thousand Oaks, New Delhi and Singapore: SAGE.

Chamberlain, B., Kasari, C. and Rotheram-Fuller, E. (2007) 'Involvement or isolation? The social networks of children with autism in regular classrooms', *Journal of Autism and Developmental Disorders*, 37: 230–42.

Conn, C. (2007) *Using Drama with Children on the Autism Spectrum*, Brackley: Speechmark.

Conn, C. (2010) *Play Better Games: Enabling Children with Autism to Join in with Everyday Games*, Milton Keynes: Speechmark.

Conn, C. (2014) *Autism and the Social World of Childhood: A Sociocultural Perspective on Theory and Practice*, Abingdon, Oxon and New York: Routledge.

Corsaro, W. A. (2011) *The Sociology of Childhood*, 3rd edn, Thousand Oaks, London and New Delhi: Pine Forge Press.

Corsaro, W. A. and Johannesen, B. O. (2007) 'The creation of new cultures in peer interaction', in J. Valsiner and A. Rosa (eds.) *The Cambridge Handbook of Sociocultural Psychology*, New York: Cambridge University Press, 444–59.

Csikszentmihalyi, M. (1992/2002) *Flow: The Classic Work on How to Achieve Happiness*, London, Sydney, Auckland and Johannesburg: Rider.

Daniels, H. (2008) *Vygotsky and Research*, London and New York: Routledge.

Davide-Rivera, J. (2012) *Twirling Naked in the Streets – And No One Noticed: Growing Up with Undiagnosed Autism*, David and Goliath Publishing.

Davidson, J. and Henderson, V. L. (2010) ' "Travel in parallel with us for a while": sensory geographies in autism', *The Canadian Geographer*, 54: 462–75.

Davidson, J. and Smith, M. (2009) 'Autistic autobiographies and more-than-human emotional geographies', *Environment and Planning D: Society and Space*, 27: 898–916.

Doody, K. R. and Mertz, J. (2013) 'Preferred play activities of children with autism spectrum disorder in a naturalistic setting', *North American Journal of Medicine and Science*, 6: 128–33.

Dunn, J. (2004) *Children's Friendships: The Beginnings of Intimacy*, Oxford: Blackwell Publishing.

Dunn, J. and Hughes, C. (2001) ' "I got some swords and you're dead!": violent fantasy, anti-social behaviour, friendship and moral sensibility in young children', *Child Development*, 72: 491–505.

Eisele, G. and Howard, J. (2012) 'Exploring the presence of characteristics associated with play within the ritual repetitive behaviour of autistic children', *International Journal of Play*, 1: 139–50.

El-Ghoroury, N. H. and Romanczyk, R. G. (1999) 'Play interactions of family members towards children with autism', *Journal of Autism and Developmental Disorders*, 29: 249–58.

Freeman, S. and Kasari, C. (2013) 'Parent-child interactions: characteristics of play', *Autism*, 17: 147–61.

Gerland, G. (1997) *A Real Person: Life on the Outside*, trans J. Tate, London: Souvenir Press.

Göncü, A. and Gaskins, S. (eds.) (2006) *Play and Development: Evolutionary, Sociocultural and Functional Perspectives*, Mahwah, NJ and London: Lawrence Erlbaum.

Goodley, D. and Runswick-Cole, K. (2010) 'Emancipating play: dis/abled children, development and deconstruction', *Disability and Society*, 25: 499–512.

Goodley, D. and Runswick-Cole, K. (2011) 'Problematising policy: conceptions of "child", "disabled" and "parents" in social policy in England', *International Journal of Inclusive Education*, 15: 71–85.

Grandin, T. and Johnson, C. (2005) *Animals in Translation: Using the Mysteries of Autism to Decode Animal Behaviour*, London: Bloomsbury.

Greenspan, S. I. and Wieder, S. (2006) *Engaging Autism: The Floortime Approach to Helping Children Relate, Communicate, and Think*, Reading, MA: Perseus Books.

Hobson, J. A., Hobson, P. R., Cheung, Y. and Caló, S. (2015) 'Symbolizing as interpersonally grounded shifts in meaning: social play in children with and without autism', *Journal of Autism and Developmental Disorders*, 45: 42–52.

Hobson, J. A., Hobson, P. R., Malik, S., Bargiota, K. and Caló, S. (2013) 'The relation between social engagement and pretend play in autism', *British Journal of Developmental Psychology*, 31: 114–27.

Hobson, R. P. (1990) 'On the origins of self and the case of autism', *Development and Psychopathology*, 2: 163–81.

Hobson, R. P. (2002) *The Cradle of Thought*, London: Macmillan.

Hobson, R. P. (2011) 'Autism and the self', in S. Gallagher (ed.) *The Oxford Handbook of the Self*, Oxford: Oxford University Press, 571–91.

Holland, P. (2003) *We Don't Play with Guns Here*, Maidenhead and Philadelphia: Open University Press.

Holmes, E. and Willoughby, T. (2005) 'Play behaviour of children with autism spectrum disorders', *Journal of Intellectual and Developmental Disability*, 30: 156–64.

Howard, J. (2002) 'Eliciting young children's perceptions of play, work and learning using the activity apperception story procedure', *Early Child Development and Care*, 172: 489–502.

Howard, J. and McInnes, K. (2013) *The Essence of Play*, London: Routledge.

Hughes, C. (2011) *Social Understanding and Social Lives: From Toddlerhood through to the Transition to School*, London and New York: Psychology Press.

Hutman, T., Siller, M. and Sigman, M. (2009) 'Mothers' narratives regarding their child with autism predict maternal synchronous behaviour during play', *Journal of Child Psychology and Psychiatry*, 50: 1255–63.

Jackson, L. (2002) *Freaks, Geeks and Asperger Syndrome: A User Guide to Adolescence*, London and New York: Jessica Kingsley Publishers.

James, A. (1993) *Childhood Identities: Self and Social Relationships in the Experience of the Child*, Edinburgh: Edinburgh University Press.

James, A. (1999) 'Learning to be friends: participant observation amongst English schoolchildren (The Midlands, England)', in C. W. Watson (ed.) *Being There: Fieldwork in Anthropology*, London and Sterling, VA: Pluto Press, 98–120.

James, A. (2013) *Socialising Children*, Basingstoke, UK, and New York: Palgrave Macmillan.

James, A., Jenks, C. and Prout, A. (1998) *Theorizing Childhood*, Cambridge, MA: Polity Press.

Jarrold, C., Boucher, J. and Smith, P. K. (1996) 'Generativity deficits in pretend play in autism', *British Journal of Developmental Psychology*, 14: 275–300.

Jarrold, C. and Conn, C. (2011) 'The development of pretend play in autism', in A. D. Pellegrini (ed.) *Oxford Handbook of the Development of Play*, New York and London: Oxford University Press, 308–21.

Jarrold, C., Smith, P., Boucher, J. and Harris, P. (1994) 'Comprehension of pretense in children with autism', *Journal of Autism and Developmental Disorders*, 24: 433–55.

Kalliala, M. (2006) *Play Culture in a Changing World*, Maidenhead: Open University Press.

Keay-Bright, W. (2009) 'ReacTickles: playful interaction with information communication technologies', *International Journal of Art and Technology*, 2: 133–51.

Kedar, I. (2012) *Ido in Autismland: Climbing Out of Autism's Silent Prison*, Sharon Kedar.

Kuhaneck, H. M. and Britner, P. A. (2013) 'A preliminary investigation of the relationship between sensory processing and social play in autism spectrum disorder', *Occupation, Participation and Health*, 33: 159–67.

Laevers, F. (1998) *The Leuven Involvement Scale for Young Children: Manual*, Leuven: Centre for Experimental Education.

Lawson, W. (2000) *Life behind Glass: A Personal Account of Autism Spectrum Disorder*, London and Philadelphia: Jessica Kingsley Publishers.

LeGoff, D. B., de la Cuesta, G. G., Krauss, G. W. and Baron-Cohen, S. (2014) *LEGO®-Based Therapy*, London and Philadelphia: Jessica Kingsley Publishers.

Leslie, A. M. (1987) 'Pretence and representation: the origins of "theory of mind"', *Psychological Review*, 94: 412–26.

Lester, S. and Russell, W. (2010) *Children's Right to Play: An Examination of the Importance of Play in the Lives of Children Worldwide. Working Papers in Early Childhood Development, No. 57*, Bernard van Leer Foundation. Online: http://files.eric.ed.gov/fulltext/ED522537.pdf (accessed 30 August 2014).

Lewis, A. and Norwich, B. (2005) *Special Teaching for Special Children? Pedagogies for Inclusion*, Maidenhead: Open University Press.

Lewis, V. and Boucher, J. (1988) 'Spontaneous, instructed and elicited play in relatively able autistic children', *British Journal of Developmental Psychology*, 6: 325–39.

Lewis, V. and Boucher, J. (1995) 'Generativity in the play of young people with autism', *Journal of Autism and Developmental Disorders*, 25: 105–21.

Libby, S., Powell, S., Messer, D. and Jordan, R. (1998) 'Spontaneous play in children with autism: a reappraisal', *Journal of Autism and Developmental Disorders*, 28: 487–97.

Lillard, A. (2006) 'Guided participation: how mothers structure and children understand pretend play', in A. Göncü and S. Gaskins (eds.) *Play and Development: Evolutionary, Sociocultural and Functional Perspectives*, Mahwah, NJ and London: Lawrence Erlbaum, 131–54.

Lillard, A. S., Lerner, M. D., Hopkins, E. J., Dore, R. A., Smith, E. D. and Palmquist, C. M. (2013) 'The impact of pretend play on children's development: a review of the evidence', *Psychological Bulletin*, 139: 1–34.

Lovaas, O. I. (2003) *Teaching Individuals with Developmental Delays: Basic Intervention Techniques*, Austin, TX: Pro-Ed.

Mastrangelo, S. (2009) 'Play and the child with autism spectrum disorder: from possibilities to practice', *International Journal of Play Therapy*, 18: 13–30.

Miller, E. and Almon, J. (2009) *Crisis in the Kindergarten: Why Children Need to Play in School*, College Park, MD: Alliance for Childhood.

Mukhopadhyay, T. R. (2008) *How Can I Talk If My Lips Don't Move?*, New York: Arcade Publishing.

Nazeer, K. (2007) *Send in the Idiots: Stories from the Other Side of Autism*, London: Bloomsbury.

Nind, M. and Hewett, D. (2005) *Access to Communication*, 2nd edn, Oxon, Abingdon and New York: David Fulton.

Ochs, E., Kremer-Sadlik, T., Sirota, K. G. and Solomon, O. (2004) 'Autism and the social world: an anthropological perspective', *Discourse Studies*, 6: 147–83.

Ochs, E. and Solomon, O. (2010) 'Autistic sociality', *Ethos*, 38: 69–92.

Panksepp, J. (2013) 'How primary-process emotional systems guide child development: ancestral regulators of human happiness, thriving, and suffering', in D. Narvaez, J. Panksepp, A. N. Schore and T. R. Gleason (eds.) *Evolution, Early Experience and Human Development: From Research to Practice and Policy*, Oxford and New York: Oxford University Press, 74–94.

Pellegrini, A. D. (2011) 'The development and function of locomotor play', in A. D. Pellegrini (ed.) *The Oxford Handbook of the Development of Play*, Oxford and New York: Oxford University Press, 172–84.

Pellegrini, A. D. and Smith, P. K. (1998) 'Physical activity play: the nature and function of a neglected aspect of play', *Child Development*, 69: 577–98.

Pellicano, E. (2012) 'The development of executive function in autism', *Autism Research and Treatment*, 1–8.

Piaget, J. (1954) *The Construction of Reality in the Child*, New York: Basic Books.

Prince-Hughes, D. (2004) *Songs of the Gorilla Nation: My Journey through Autism*, New York: Three Rivers Press.

Prizant, B. M., Wetherby, A. M., Rubin, E., Laurent, A. C. and Rydell, P. J. (2006) *The SCERTS Model: A Comprehensive Educational Approach for Children with Autism Spectrum Disorders. Volume II: Program Planning and Intervention*, Baltimore, MD: Paul H. Brookes Publishing Co.

Prout, A. (2005) *The Future of Childhood: Towards the Interdisciplinary Study of Children*, London and New York: Routledge.

Qvortrup, J. (1994) 'Childhood matters: an introduction', in J. Qvortrup, M. Bardy, G. Sgritta and H. Wintersberger (eds.) *Childhood Matters: Social Theory, Practice and Politics*, Aldershot: Avebury Press, 1–23.

Rogers, S. J. and Dawson, G. (2010) *Early Start Denver Model for Young Children with Autism: Promoting Language, Learning and Engagement*, New York: Guilford Press.

Rogers, S. J. and Ozonoff, S. (2005) 'What do we know about sensory dysfunction in autism? A critical review of the empirical evidence', *Journal of Child Psychology and Psychiatry*, 46: 1255–68.

Seach, D. (2007) *Interactive Play for Children with Autism*, London and New York: Routledge.

Sinclair, J. (2005) *Autism Network International: The Development of a Community and Its Culture*. Online: http://www.autreat.com/History_of_ANI.html (accessed 29 September 2014).

Sinclair, J. (2009) *Why I Dislike "Person First" Language*. Online: http://autismmythbusters. com/general-public/autistic-vs-people-with-autism/jim-sinclair-why-i-dislike-person-first-language/ (accessed 17 August 2015).

Singer, J. (1999) ' "Why can't you be normal for once in your life?" From a "problem with no name" to the emergence of a new category of difference', in M. Corker and S. French (eds.) *Disability Discourse*, Buckingham: Open University Press, 59–67.

Siraj-Blatchford, I., Sylva, K., Muttock, S., Gilden, R. and Bell, D. (2002) *Researching Effective Pedagogy in the Early Years: DFES Research Report 356*, London: Department of Education and Skills, HMSO.

Sluss, D. J. (2014) *Supporting Play in Early Childhood: Environment, Curriculum, Assessment*, 2nd edn, Stamford, CT: Cengage Learning.

Stern, D. N. (1985) *The Interpersonal World of the Infant*, New York: Basic Books.

Straus, J. N. (2013) 'Autism as culture', in L. J. Davis (ed.) *The Disability Studies Reader*, 4th edn, New York and Abingdon, Oxon: Routledge, 460–84.

Striano, T., Tomasello, M. and Rochat, P. (2001) 'Social and object support for early symbolic play', *Developmental Science*, 4: 442–55.

Sturrock, G. and Else, P. (1998/2005) 'The playground as therapeutic space: playwork as healing (The Colorado Paper)', in P. Else (ed.) *Therapeutic Playwork Reader One*, Southampton: Common Threads.

Sutton-Smith, B. (1997) *The Ambiguity of Play*, Cambridge, MA and London: Harvard University Press.

Tammet, D. (2006) *Born on a Blue Day: A Memoir of Asperger's and an Extraordinary Mind*, London: Hodder.

Taylor, M. (1999) *Imaginary Companions and the Children Who Create Them*, New York and Oxford: Oxford University Press.

Theodorou, F. and Nind, M. (2010) 'Inclusion in play: a case study of a child with autism in an inclusive nursery', *Journal of Research in Special Educational Needs*, 10: 99–106.

Tomasello, M., Striano, T. and Rochat, P. (1999) 'Do young children use objects as symbols?', *British Journal of Developmental Psychology*, 17: 563–84.

Trevarthen, C. and Daniel, S. (2006) *Rhythm and Synchrony in Early Development, and Signs of Autism and Rett Syndrome in Infancy*. Paper presented at AWARES.org Autism2006 Conference, 2 October. Online: http://awares.org/conferences/show_paper.asp?section=00010001 0001&conferenceCode=000200020014&id=64&full_paper=1 (accessed 12 October 2014).

UN General Assembly (1989) *Convention on the Rights of the Child*, Document A/RES/44/25 (12 December), New York: United Nations.

VanFleet, R. and Colțea, C. (2012) 'Helping children with ASD through canine-assisted play therapy', in L. Gallo-Lopez and L. C. Rubin (eds.) *Play-based Interventions for Children and Adolescents with Autism Spectrum Disorders*, New York and London: Routledge, 39–72.

Vygotsky, L. S. (1978) *Mind in Society*, Cambridge, MA: Harvard University Press.

Waite, S. and Pratt, N. (2011) 'Theoretical perspectives on learning outside the classroom: relationships between learning and place', in S. Waite (ed.) *Children Learning Outside the Classroom: From Birth to Eleven*, Los Angeles, London, New Delhi, Singapore and Washington, DC: SAGE, 1–18.

Willett, R. (2013) 'An overview of games and activities on two primary school playgrounds', in R. Willett, C. Richards, J. Marsh, A. Burn and J. Bishop (eds.) *Children, Media and Playground Cultures: Ethnographic Studies of School Playtimes*, New York: Palgrave Macmillan, 21–50.

Williams, D. (1992) *Nobody Nowhere*, London: Corgi.

Williams, D. (2008) Conference discussion (Psychology), AWARES.org Autism2008 Conference. Online: http://www.awares.org/conferences/show_paper.asp?section=000100010001&conferenceCode=000200100012&id=194&full_paper=1 (accessed 10 December 2008).

Williams, E., Reddy, V. and Costall, A. (2001) 'Taking a closer look at functional play in children with autism', *Journal of Autism and Developmental Disorders*, 31: 67–77.

Wimpory, D. C. and Nash, S. (1999) 'Musical interaction therapy: therapeutic play for children with autism', *Child Language Teaching and Therapy*, 15: 17–28.

Winnicott, D. W. (1971) *Playing and Reality*, London: Tavistock.

Wolfberg, P. J. (1999) *Play and Imagination in Children with Autism*, New York and London: Teachers College.

Wolfberg, P., DeWitt, M., Young, G. S. and Nguyen, T. (2015) 'Integrated play groups: promoting symbolic play and social engagement with typical peers in children with ASD across settings', *Journal of Autism and Developmental Disorders*, 45: 830–45.

Woodhead, M. (2005) 'Early childhood development: a question of rights', *International Journal of Early Childhood*, 37: 79–98.

Woolley, H., Armitage, M., Bishop, J. C., Curtis, M. and Ginsborg, J. (2005) *Inclusion of Disabled Children in Primary School Playgrounds*, London: National Children's Bureau.

Index